# Time Efficiency Makeover

# Time Efficiency Makeover

*Own your time and
your life by conquering
procrastination*

*Organizing for a better
quality of life*

Dorothy K. Breininger
Debby S. Bitticks

Health Communications, Inc.
Deerfield Beach, Florida

*www.bcibooks.com*

The purpose of this book is to inspire. The information in this book is provided with the understanding that the authors, and publishers and their related companies, directors, employees, partners and agents are not engaged in rendering medical, legal, accounting, tax, or other professional advice and services. As such, this book should not be used as a substitute for consultation with professional, medical, accounting, tax, legal or other competent advisers.

**Library of Congress Cataloging-in-Publication Data is available from the Library of Congress**

©2005 Debby S. Bitticks and Dorothy K. Breininger.
ISBN 0-7573-0350-1

Publisher: Health Communications, Inc.
          3201 S.W. 15th Street
          Deerfield Beach, FL 33442-8190

*Cover design by Karen Ross www.beitnow.com*

*"Procrastination is the fear of success. People procrastinate because they are afraid of the success that they know will result if they move ahead now. Because success is heavy, carries a responsibility with it, it is much easier to procrastinate and live on the 'someday I'll' philosophy."*
—Dennis Waitley

Dedicated to our clients (our teachers) who brought forth their time management dilemmas and allowed us the opportunity to find the answers together with them.

# Contents

*"Much of the stress that people feel doesn't come from having too much to do. It comes from not finishing what they started."*
—David Allen

**Acknowledgments** . . . . . . . . . . . . . . . . . . . . . . . . . . . . . . . . ix

**Introduction** . . . . . . . . . . . . . . . . . . . . . . . . . . . . . . . . . . . . . xi

**What Is Procrastination?** . . . . . . . . . . . . . . . . . . . . . . . . . . . 1

**Why Does Procrastination Happen?** . . . . . . . . . . . . . . . . . . . 3

**How Can I Begin to Change?** . . . . . . . . . . . . . . . . . . . . . . . 17

**Am I A Procrastinator?** . . . . . . . . . . . . . . . . . . . . . . . . . . . . 59
- Personal Finances . . . . . . . . . . . . . . . . . . . . . . . . . . . . . . 60
- Office . . . . . . . . . . . . . . . . . . . . . . . . . . . . . . . . . . . . . . . 72
- Relationships . . . . . . . . . . . . . . . . . . . . . . . . . . . . . . . . . 88
- Travel . . . . . . . . . . . . . . . . . . . . . . . . . . . . . . . . . . . . . . 96
- Living Area . . . . . . . . . . . . . . . . . . . . . . . . . . . . . . . . . . 101
- Medical Issues . . . . . . . . . . . . . . . . . . . . . . . . . . . . . . . 111
- Study Issues . . . . . . . . . . . . . . . . . . . . . . . . . . . . . . . . . 118
- Personal and House Errands . . . . . . . . . . . . . . . . . . . . . 125

**Tools for Change** . . . . . . . . . . . . . . . . . . . . . . . . . . . . . . . . 133
**Forms for Change** . . . . . . . . . . . . . . . . . . . . . . . . . . . . . . . 139
**Resources** . . . . . . . . . . . . . . . . . . . . . . . . . . . . . . . . . . . . . 157

# Acknowledgments

*"Tomorrow is the only day in the year that appeals to a lazy man."*
—Jimmy Lyons

Thank You!  Thank You!  Thank You!  Thank You!

If only . . .

If only I had more time. If only I had started earlier. If only I had asked more questions, been more organized, had more money, called in advance, admitted I was overwhelmed . . . If only . . . If only I had purchased *Time Efficiency Makeover*. Well, you have.  Pick a page and start.  Avoid perfection. Welcome success.

This path to success has been created for you by amazing organizers, writers, assistants, and even procrastinators. It is with absolute admiration that each member of the Time Efficiency Makeover Team met each request and delay. We indeed want to share with the world how each and every contributor is important to the creation of this binder.

**Jerry Krautman, Lead Researcher and Editor**
**Gillian Drake, Project Manager**

Abdelmonem A. Afifi, Ph.D. and Dean Emeritus, UCLA

Chris Faltynek, Office Manager, Los Angeles Office

Lynn Benson, President Delphi Health Products, Inc.

David Factor, Company Business Consultant

David P. Boyd, III, Ph.D. and Dean Emeritus, Northeastern University

Dr. Phil McGraw, Dr. Phil Show

Edd Brady, Manager, Wisconsin Office

Jeff Scott, Content Media Group

Jerry Gutterman, Gutterman Consulting

Joy Nash, Assistant to Dorothy

Karen Ross, Be It Now, K.G. Ross Inc.

Ken Bitticks, Debby's husband, her children and grandchildren

Marty and Judy Feldman, CEO, Values Down Under

Nader (Ben) Afram, PostNet and Business Services

NAPO (National Association of Professional Organizers)

Pat Brady, Technical Editor

Phil Lobel, President, Lobeline Communications

Rick Cataldo, President DENOVO Medical Venture Marketing

Ruth and Robert Breininger, Dorothy's parents

Selma Schimmel, Debby's sister

Sharma Bennett, Marriage and Family Therapist

Anthony Robbins, CEO, Anthony Robbins Foundation

Jack Canfield and Patty Aubery, Self-Esteem Seminars, Inc.

Tracey and Kathy Krueger, Challenge Graphics

Von and Jill Varga, clients

# Introduction

*"This is as true in everyday life as it is in battle: we are given one life and the decision is ours whether to wait for circumstances to make up our mind, or whether to act, and in acting, to live."*

**—General Omar Bradley**

You can't put it off any longer!

That is what this workbook is all about. Taking action now. Not putting off your life any longer.

Procrastination is a learned activity and this workbook is going to help you unlearn it.

We have designed this workbook to be interactive. In every section you will find information about procrastination, and you will also find opportunities for integrating new ways of being.

You will be able to ask yourself:

- Does this definition of procrastination agree with my own experience and understanding?
- Have I felt this emotion in this way before?
- Have I experienced this lack of motivation or resistance to a task before?
- Have I been in this situation before?
- How have I successfully dealt with similar situations before?

This workbook is yours. No one else will have access to it. So, be as honest with yourself as possible. The questions and situations presented here are to help you think about your life and the kinds of daily agreements you make with yourself. These questions can only help you if you confront the information and questions openly.

We hope you find insights about yourself and that the **Tools for Change** and **Forms for Change** sections give you concrete ways to organize your life.

So don't put it off any longer. Read the information, answer the questions and unlock your very own answers.

And most important, be good to yourself. It took years to learn to become a procrastinator; it is going to take some time to unlearn it. The secret is to take action—now.

# What Is Procrastination?

*"How wonderful it is that nobody need wait a single moment before starting to improve the world."*

—Anne Frank

"Procrastinate" is a verb meaning *"to put off intentionally the doing of something that should be done."*

Procrastination is as common as there are people on earth. Everyone procrastinates at one time or another. Procrastination is a habit, not a fatal flaw. It is probably the single most common hindrance to effective time management. It takes persistence to change, but you can do it.

Very simply stated, procrastination is the deliberate act of excessive postponing. How much trouble your postponing causes depends to a large degree on the "price you have to pay" for that behavior.

Procrastination is the avoidance of doing a task that needs to be accomplished. This avoidance can lead to feelings of guilt, inadequacy, depression and self-doubt. Procrastination has a high potential for painful consequences. It interferes with professional, academic and personal success. Psychologist William Knaus estimates that 90 percent of college students procrastinate. Of these students, 25 percent are chronic procrastinators and this group is usually the one who ends up dropping out of college.

## Not A Time Management Problem
According to Joseph Ferrari, Ph.D., Associate Professor of Psychology at De Paul University in Chicago, procrastination is not a time management or planning problem. Procrastinators do not differ in their ability to estimate time, however they may be more optimistic in their ability to complete tasks. "Telling someone who procrastinates to buy a weekly planner is like telling someone with chronic depression to just cheer up," insists Dr. Ferrari.

## It's A Shift In Priorities
In addition, fear can be a driving force for procrastination. For example, we may worry that we can't pay our bills next month and begin to work overtime to compensate for that financial shortfall. Suddenly, tasks at home to which we've committed, don't get done and, sadly, we are incorrectly labeled procrastinators. A whole new pattern begins and eventually we do fall victim to the label.

So now you know what it is. Find out why it happens.

Don't wait to find out, turn the page now.

# Why Does Procrastination Happen?

*"Never leave that till tomorrow which you can do today."*
—Benjamin Franklin

***Procrastinators can successfully change the way they live their lives.***

From our previous section we know that procrastination is the *deliberate act of excessive postponing*. But what are the underlying reasons why people procrastinate? We have organized this section into a series of statements and their explanations. Please read them carefully.

In the following exercise, you will find:

- Examples of common phrases or "excuses" procrastinators use.
- Supporting "quotes" about the phrases listed.
- Explanations of the procrastination phrases listed.
- Sections for you to respond with your own experience in relationship to the particular "excuses."

*Please take the time to explore these sections. They are there to help understand how procrastination affects you.*

### How Procrastination Works Inside Your Head

A task is a task. It is our "feeling" toward the *task* that may cause us to procrastinate. Everyday we are confronted with **tasks**, whether they are writing a paper, cleaning the garage or paying our bills. Inside our heads we deal with **feelings** about the task that guide what we do. If those feelings are negative, we may put off the task. The result is we can use our feelings to deal with the task rationally or irrationally. The rational voice says, "I hate cleaning the garage, but because company is coming this weekend, I'd better get to it now. You never know what might come up before then." The irrational voice says, "I hate cleaning the garage and this task is just too big. I have company coming this weekend, but I can avoid taking them in the garage and really, summer is a much better time to be dealing with it."

### Feelings of Inadequacy

According to Sharma Bennett, a licensed psychotherapist practicing in Los Angeles, the act of procrastination is also the act of postponing the actualization of one's potential. Fear-based, these cluttered thoughts distract one from the deeper issues of life. The continued act of procrastination can result in feelings of worthlessness and inadequacy.

# Why Does Procrastination Happen?

*"Do you know what happens when you give a procrastinator a good idea? Nothing!"*

—Donald Gardner

Here is a list of common procrastinator phrases and the *feelings* that lie underneath:

- **"I know I can't do this."**
- **We certainly live up to our expectations.**

    If you think that you can't do a task, you won't be able to. If you think that you are worthless, unloved, or unchangeable, you will feel depressed and unmotivated. It's time to change the phrase to "I know I can do this."

    I've said this about a project I was working on.      ☐ Yes      ☐ No

    I've procrastinated on the project using this statement.      ☐ Yes      ☐ No

    Name a specific task or project where you used this excuse and list some details or reasons why you either did or did not procrastinate:

    _____

    _____

    _____

    _____

- **"This stuff is just plain boring."**
- **Even the *Starship Enterprise* had to do star mapping.**

    Sometimes the task has little importance to your life or work; it might be "busy work." If something is neither important nor meaningful to you personally, it may be difficult to get motivated to begin the task. Create a meaningful thought for the task and begin.

    I've said this about a project I was working on.      ☐ Yes      ☐ No

    I've procrastinated on the project using this statement.      ☐ Yes      ☐ No

    Name a specific task or project where you used this excuse and list some details or reasons why you either did or did not procrastinate:

    _____

    _____

    _____

    _____

# Why Does Procrastination Happen?

*"Even if you're on the right track—you'll get run over if you just sit there."*
—Arthur Godfrey

- **"The task is just too big."**
- **Looking at the forest and not the trees.**

  Analyze the project as a series of tasks and not one large one. Try to realistically figure out how long it takes to complete the sub-tasks (trees). Break down large projects into at least five smaller, more manageable sections and work on them one at a time.

  I've said this about a project I was working on.  ☐ Yes ☐ No
  I've procrastinated on the project using this statement. ☐ Yes ☐ No
  Name a specific task or project where you used this excuse and list some details or reasons why you either did or did not procrastinate:

  _____

  _____

  _____

  _____

- **"The task will take a long time to complete."**
- **Your mother always said, "Take small bites and chew slowly."**

  Similar to the trees, only this time the task may take longer than you have assigned and may impinge on other activities.

  I've said this about a project I was working on.  ☐ Yes ☐ No
  I've procrastinated on the project using this statement. ☐ Yes ☐ No
  Name a specific task or project where you used this excuse and list some details or reasons why you either did or did not procrastinate:

  _____

  _____

  _____

  _____

# Why Does Procrastination Happen?

*"Don't wait. The time will never be just right."*

—Napoleon Hill

- "I can't get started."
- **Ninety percent of getting started is "showing up!"**
  The hardest part of running or working out is getting out the door. Once you get going, your heart starts pumping and you make progress. Break large projects into smaller, more manageable sections and work on them one at a time. Even when you don't feel like it, just take one tiny small step—just one.

  I've said this about a project I was working on.        ☐ Yes        ☐ No
  I've procrastinated on the project using this statement. ☐ Yes        ☐ No
  Name a specific task or project where you used this excuse and list some details or reasons why you either did or did not procrastinate:

  _____

  _____

  _____

  _____

- "I am busy doing so many things I can't concentrate on the task at hand."
- **The power of focus is essential for task completion.**
  Your time is so filled that you don't have time to complete other important tasks. Or, maybe you were not able to prioritize the time effectively. Ask yourself "what is my most important task today?"

  I've said this about a project I was working on.        ☐ Yes        ☐ No
  I've procrastinated on the project using this statement. ☐ Yes        ☐ No
  Name a specific task or project where you used this excuse and list some details or reasons why you either did or did not procrastinate:

  _____

  _____

  _____

  _____

# Why Does Procrastination Happen?

*"When you have to make a choice and don't make it, that in itself is a choice."*
—William James

- "I have no ownership of this task."
- **Nobody cares about my opinion.**

  If a project is given to you and you had no input in the construction of the task, you may not want to spend time on the project. If you find yourself in this situation repeatedly, you might consider discussing it with the person who has given you these "ownerless" tasks, or seek other work. Consistently doing someone else's "to dos" will sap your motivation over time.

  I've said this about a project I was working on.　　　　　□ Yes　　□ No

  I've procrastinated on the project using this statement.　　□ Yes　　□ No

  Name a specific task or project where you used this excuse and list some details or reasons why you either did or did not procrastinate:

  _____

  _____

  _____

  _____

- "I'm afraid I will mess this up."
- **"We have nothing to fear but fear itself."** —President Franklin Roosevelt

  You are afraid that your friends and colleagues will know that you are a failure if you "mess up" the assignment. You may think you are in over your head. Predicting this outcome can be immobilizing. Let's create a positive outcome.

  I've said this about a project I was working on.　　　　　□ Yes　　□ No

  I've procrastinated on the project using this statement.　□ Yes　　□ No

  Name a specific task or project where you used this excuse and list some details or reasons why you either did or did not procrastinate:

  _____

  _____

  _____

  _____

# Why Does Procrastination Happen?

*"You may delay, but time will not."*

—Benjamin Franklin

- **"I shouldn't have to do this; it's not fair."**
- **"Redirect the substantial energy of your frustration and turn it into positive, effective, unstoppable determination." —Ralph Marston**

  You assume that you should be able to solve your problems and reach your goals rapidly and easily. Rather than being patient and persistent when life gets tough, you may rebel against the "unfairness" of it all and give up completely.

  I've said this about a project I was working on.　　　☐ Yes　　☐ No
  I've procrastinated on the project using this statement.　　☐ Yes　　☐ No
  Name a specific task or project where you used this excuse and list some details or reasons why you either did or did not procrastinate:

  _____

  _____

  _____

  _____

- **"I don't know how to do this."**
- **If you don't speak French you won't know to *ouvrez la fenêtre* (open the window) when asked.**

  If you lack training, skill, ability or access to the resources to do the job, you may avoid the task completely. Seek out the knowledge in order to complete the task.

  I've said this about a project I was working on.　　　☐ Yes　　☐ No
  I've procrastinated on the project using this statement.　　☐ Yes　　☐ No
  Name a specific task or project where you used this excuse and list some details or reasons why you either did or did not procrastinate:

  _____

  _____

  _____

  _____

# Why Does Procrastination Happen?

*"Delay always breeds danger; and to protract a great design is often to ruin it."*

—Miguel De Cervantes

- "I need to do things perfectly."
- "Every time, all the time, I'm a perfectionist. I feel I should never lose."
  **—Chris Evert-Lloyd**

  You stop even before you start. Because you will settle for nothing less than perfection, you make the task more difficult than it has to be. You end up avoiding the task and procrastinating. Instead, avoid perfection-at-all-costs and finish the project.

  I've said this about a project I was working on.      ☐ Yes      ☐ No
  I've procrastinated on the project using this statement.      ☐ Yes      ☐ No
  Name a specific task or project where you used this excuse and list some details or reasons why you either did or did not procrastinate:

  _____

  _____

  _____

  _____

- "I don't know if my boss or teacher will like my work."
- **You are afraid of what those with power will think.**

  Projecting other people's responses can really divert or stifle our creative process. It's okay to make mistakes—mistakes can be fixed. Missing a deadline, flunking out or losing a job cannot.

  I've said this about a project I was working on.      ☐ Yes      ☐ No
  I've procrastinated on the project using this statement.      ☐ Yes      ☐ No
  Name a specific task or project where you used this excuse and list some details or reasons why you either did or did not procrastinate:

  _____

  _____

  _____

  _____

9

# Why Does Procrastination Happen?

*"It is an undoubted truth, that the less one has to do, the less time one finds to do it in."*

—Lord Chesterfield

- **"I'm not sure what the task is."**
- **If you are not sure what is expected of you, it may be difficult to get started.**
  Often we try to "guess" the expectation of a task and we begin based on that assumption. It can be very frustrating to find yourself half way through a task and be going down the wrong path entirely. Next time, if you don't know, ask.

I've said this about a project I was working on.          ☐ Yes     ☐ No
I've procrastinated on the project using this statement.     ☐ Yes     ☐ No
Name a specific task or project where you used this excuse and list some details or reasons why you either did or did not procrastinate:

_____

_____

_____

- **"This task is too difficult."**
- **"Why do we choose to go to the moon? Not because it is easy but because it is hard." —President John F. Kennedy**
  We naturally tend to avoid difficult things in favor of those that seem easy to us. It may be difficult to get started if you think it is too difficult for you. It's time to reframe your thinking and train your brain to believe how easy this task is.

I've said this about a project I was working on.          ☐ Yes     ☐ No
I've procrastinated on the project using this statement.     ☐ Yes     ☐ No
Name a specific task or project where you used this excuse and list some details or reasons why you either did or did not procrastinate:

_____

_____

_____

# Why Does Procrastination Happen?

*"There are a million ways to lose a work day, but not even a single way to get one back."*

—Tom DeMarco and Timothy Lister

- "I've never done this before."
- **Pride comes from accomplishment. Pride and self growth come from trying new things. Pride and self growth increase our own self image. Positive self image replaces fear.**

  It is the fear of the unknown. When doing something for the first time, you have no way of knowing how well you will do. We desire comfort in familiar things and this may delay your beginning the task.

  I've said this about a project I was working on.      ☐ Yes    ☐ No
  I've procrastinated on the project using this statement.      ☐ Yes    ☐ No
  Name a specific task or project where you used this excuse and list some details or reasons why you either did or did not procrastinate:

  _____

  _____

  _____

  _____

- "I'm not good at anything."
- **Negative thinking will enforce negative outcomes. If you think you can't; you won't.**

  Try acting "as if" you are great at doing the task at hand—eventually, you will be.

  I've said this about a project I was working on.      ☐ Yes    ☐ No
  I've procrastinated on the project using this statement.      ☐ Yes    ☐ No
  Name a specific task or project where you used this excuse and list some details or reasons why you either did or did not procrastinate:

  _____

  _____

  _____

  _____

# Why Does Procrastination Happen?

*"Procrastination is one of the most common and deadliest of diseases and its toll on success and happiness is heavy."*

—Wayne Dyer

- **"I'm angry that I have to do this task."**
- **Sometimes we get angry because we are being forced to do something we don't want to do. Procrastination can be a passive aggressive way of dealing with it.**

  We have the choice from minute to minute as to which mood or emotion we allow ourselves to experience. We have the power to change our thoughts and moods, so we can move through those emotions and create forward movement on our task. Creating a mantra to replace the feeling of anger can help.

  I've said this about a project I was working on.　　☐ Yes　　☐ No

  I've procrastinated on the project using this statement.　　☐ Yes　　☐ No

  Name a specific task or project where you used this excuse and list some details or reasons why you either did or did not procrastinate:

  _____

  _____

  _____

- **"I'd rather be doing something else."**
- **Yes, the grass always seems greener on the other side of the fence.**

  There are a lot of other things we feel we should be doing. We may be more focused on those tasks than on the one at hand. This can be addressed by defining our goals. When we have goals, we can select tasks that support our goals and feel a sense of confidence that what we're working on is meaningful.

  I've said this about a project I was working on.　　☐ Yes　　☐ No

  I've procrastinated on the project using this statement.　　☐ Yes　　☐ No

  Name a specific task or project where you used this excuse and list some details or reasons why you either did or did not procrastinate:

  _____

  _____

  _____

# Why Does Procrastination Happen?

*"Procrastination is a sin of lawyers, trial judges, reporters, appellate judges, in brief, everyone connected with the machinery of criminal law."*
—Macklin Fleming

- "I have bigger fish to fry."
- Picture a little snowball rolling down a hill—eventually it grows larger and larger and disaster strikes.

  You have other personal problems such as financial difficulties or problems with your interpersonal relationships. This is all about integrity—if you disregard the small agreements with yourself and others, your view of yourself will deteriorate; thus, creating more and bigger problems (fish). Be sure to give respect to the little fish (agreements) and keep your self-worth intact.

  I've said this about a project I was working on.     ☐ Yes    ☐ No
  I've procrastinated on the project using this statement.    ☐ Yes    ☐ No
  Name a specific task or project where you used this excuse and list some details or reasons why you either did or did not procrastinate:

  _____

  _____

  _____

- "I can't get any work done around here."
- How can I prepare dinner if the kitchen isn't clean? How can I repair my motorcycle if my tools aren't in order?

  It's kind of tough to paint a painting on top of an existing painting. It's necessary to have a blank canvas to create your new painting. When you sit at your desk and you find yourself daydreaming, staring into space, doodling or checking your e-mail every other minute the reasons may be: your work area is distracting and noisy, your desk is cluttered and disorganized or you are in areas that aren't conducive to work.

  I've said this about a project I was working on.     ☐ Yes    ☐ No
  I've procrastinated on the project using this statement.    ☐ Yes    ☐ No
  Name a specific task or project where you used this excuse and list some details or reasons why you either did or did not procrastinate:

  _____

  _____

  _____

# Why Does Procrastination Happen?

*"Know the true value of time; snatch, seize, and enjoy every moment of it. No idleness; no laziness; no procrastination; never put off till tomorrow what you can do today."*

—Lord Chesterfield

- **"I'm too tired."**
- **Driving a car on an empty gas tank won't get you very far.**

    Psychological and physical fatigue have the same effect. Your mind and body need to be rested and sharp to meet the challenges of the day. You are fighting your fatigue along with the task at hand. Increase your chances of success by getting six to nine hours of sleep or by taking a midday nap.

    I've said this about a project I was working on.     ☐ Yes    ☐ No
    I've procrastinated on the project using this statement.    ☐ Yes    ☐ No
    Name a specific task or project where you used this excuse and list some details or reasons why you either did or did not procrastinate:

    _____

    _____

    _____

- **"I have too many things to do."**
- **Living in a state of "overwhelm" is the new American way—not *the* way—but the American Way.**

    You aren't managing your priorities effectively. If you consider everything a priority, nothing is a priority. You must come to terms with the idea that there's just too much stuff, information, and projects. With computers at your fingertips, you are empowered to do everything from downloading your bank statements to "developing and sizing" your photos. Remember, just because you can, doesn't mean you have to.

    I've said this about a project I was working on.     ☐ Yes    ☐ No
    I've procrastinated on the project using this statement.    ☐ Yes    ☐ No
    Name a specific task or project where you used this excuse and list some details or reasons why you either did or did not procrastinate:

    _____

    _____

    _____

# Why Does Procrastination Happen?

*"I don't wait for moods. You accomplish nothing if you do that. Your mind must know it has got to get down to work."*

—Pearl S. Buck

- **The Stages in the Cycle of Procrastination:**
  **Example: A manager struggles with the task of writing the semi-annual personnel report.**

| | |
|---|---|
| "I'll get an early start this time." | *But now isn't the right time.* |
| "I've really got to start soon." | *There's still lots of time.* |
| "What if I don't start the project on time?" | *Feeling the pressure of the consequences.* |
| "I should have started sooner." | *Starting to feel guilty.* |
| "I am doing my filing, I've checked my e-mail, but the report…" | *At least I did something "productive."* |
| "I can never enjoy going out with friends." | *The procrastinator tries to enjoy other activities but the report keeps her from relaxing and enjoying her friends and fun.* |
| "Hey, there is still time to finish it." | *The deadline is approaching, but hope springs eternal.* |
| "There must be something wrong with me." | *The procrastinator gets down on herself and intensifies the cycle.* |
| "Why bother—there is no way I can finish it" or "I can't put it off any longer." | *The choice is finally made. It is either blown off as not worth the effort or it is finally completed with the realization that it wasn't all that bad, "but I should have started earlier."* |
| "I will never do this to myself again." | *If the price is high enough, the procrastinator might start making the changes required. If not, the cycle begins again.* |

# How Can I Begin to Change?

*"Procrastination has robbed us of too many opportunities."*

—Sarah Ban Breathnach

So far we have established a working definition of procrastination, we understand some of the underlying reasons behind it and we know if we are procrastinators and if so, in what areas we procrastinate the most. The following section will give you concrete help in overcoming your procrastination issues.

Please notice that after each informational paragraph we have provided a section for you to analyze how the statement either applies or doesn't apply to you. *If you take the time to see how the statements affect you, you will be well on your way to understanding how to beat procrastination for yourself.*

*As you review this section, pay special attention to the statements that will be most beneficial to you. Select at least ten statements and focus your energy on those top ten.*

# ow Can I Begin to Change?

*"The way to get started is to quit talking and begin doing."*

—Walt Disney

## Psychological Factors

- **Pinpoint the Fear**

  What is preventing you from doing what you need to do? Is pain stopping you from going to the dentist? Are you afraid of failure? There are many fears out there; the trick is to determine what is holding you back and working to overcome it. Also, *knowing* what you need to do will give you the confidence to complete the task. The more you understand what it is you are to do, the easier it will be to do it. Know yourself, know your fears, and know the task ahead in order to succeed.

  ☐ Yes ☐ No This applies to me.

  Here are some details about how it applies to me:

  _____

  _____

  _____

  _____

  _____

  Here are two small ways I can move forward successfully:

  _____

  _____

  _____

  _____

  _____

# How Can I Begin to Change?

*"The time to repair the roof is when the sun is shining."*

—John F. Kennedy

- **Stop Trying to Be So Perfect**

  "Satisfize" don't optimize. You can refine it later. If you wait for all circumstances to be in order, you may never begin the task.

  ☐ Yes   ☐ No  This applies to me.
  Here are some details about how it applies to me:

  _____

  _____

  _____

  _____

  _____

  Here are two small ways I can move forward successfully:

  _____

  _____

  _____

  _____

  _____

# How Can I Begin to Change?

*"Delays have dangerous ends."*

—William Shakespeare

- **Are You Depressed?**

It's easy to procrastinate if you're feeling depressed. Fight to remember all the wonderful things you can do. As Stuart Smalley used to say, "I'm smart enough. I'm good enough and gosh darn it, people like me." You need to believe in yourself. You'll find that you will get more done when you have a positive attitude about yourself.

☐ Yes   ☐ No  This applies to me.

Here are some details about how it applies to me:

_____

_____

_____

_____

_____

Here are two small ways I can move forward successfully:

_____

_____

_____

_____

_____

# How Can I Begin to Change?

*"Never put off till tomorrow what you can do today."*

—Thomas Jefferson

- **Think Positive Thoughts**

  Negative thoughts will sap your intellectual, emotional and physical strength. But you have a defense against it. Think *positive*. If you think that the world is against you and failure is around the corner, you will not be able to begin the task ahead. You are bright and perceptive enough to understand that procrastination is a problem for you. Otherwise you would not be reading this book. You are half way there. Thinking positively will boost you, and enable you to meet your goals.

  ☐ Yes   ☐ No  This applies to me.
  Here are some details about how it applies to me:

  _____

  _____

  _____

  _____

  _____


  Here are two small ways I can move forward successfully:

  _____

  _____

  _____

  _____

  _____

# How Can I Begin to Change?

*"Procrastination is opportunity's natural assassin."*

—Victor Kiam

- **Decide on Your Long-Range Goals**

  Long-range goal setting is a great way of framing your priorities and daily to-dos. Amplify them by reciting them to yourself as well as writing them, which will encourage you throughout the day.

  ☐ Yes   ☐ No  This applies to me.
  Here are some details about how it applies to me:

  _____

  _____

  _____

  _____

  _____

  Here are two small ways I can move forward successfully:

  _____

  _____

  _____

  _____

  _____

# How Can I Begin to Change?

*"My evil genius Procrastination has whispered me to tarry 'til a more convenient season."*

—Mary Todd Lincoln

## Time Management

- **Compare Today's Tasks with Your Larger Goals**
  Be sure you select the tasks which fall in line and support your goals. Analyze your goals and see if the task you set will further those goals.

  ☐ Yes   ☐ No  This applies to me.
  Here are some details about how it applies to me:

  _____

  _____

  _____

  _____

  _____

  Here are two small ways I can move forward successfully:

  _____

  _____

  _____

  _____

  _____

# How Can I Begin to Change?

*"While we deliberate about beginning it is already too late to begin."*
—Marcus Fabius Quintilianus

- **Set Reachable and Specific Sub-Goals**
  For instance, "Read twenty pages of chapter 5 by 8:00 tonight," rather than "Do some studying later." This helps you gain a sense of accomplishment from having reached your goal.

  ☐ Yes   ☐ No  This applies to me.
  Here are some details about how it applies to me:

  _____

  _____

  _____

  _____

  _____

  Here are two small ways I can move forward successfully:

  _____

  _____

  _____

  _____

# How Can I Begin to Change?

*" . . .who waits until circumstances completely favor his undertaking, will never accomplish anything."*

—Martin Luther

- **Think in Terms of Committed Time Slots**

  Commit yourself to spending a "block" of time working on an unpleasant task rather than an "amount" of work to be done. Your commitment is to the time. You may choose to do nothing if you wish, but you may find that the task itself becomes less unpleasant (knowing you are only committed to working on it for a half hour) rather than doing nothing at all.

  ☐ Yes ☐ No This applies to me.

  Here are some details about how it applies to me:

  _____

  _____

  _____

  _____

  _____

  Here are two small ways I can move forward successfully:

  _____

  _____

  _____

  _____

  _____

# How Can I Begin to Change?

*"Slaying the dragon of delay is no sport for the short-winded."*
—Sandra Day O'Connor

- **Use Odd Time As an Ally**
  Ten minutes while waiting for a friend or a ride can be used to jot notes about a paper or sketch a plan for a project. Don't expect to get it all done in one sitting.

  ☐ Yes  ☐ No  This applies to me.
  Here are some details about how it applies to me:

  _____

  _____

  _____

  _____

  _____

  Here are two small ways I can move forward successfully:

  _____

  _____

  _____

  _____

  _____

# How Can I Begin to Change?

*"Procrastination is like a credit card: it's a lot of fun until you get the bill."*
—Christopher Parker

## Organize Your Space

- **You Can't Work, If You Can't Find Anything**
  Organize your work area, including your tools, so you won't have a chance to procrastinate. Arrange your desk just the way you like it, and work at times when you have peak energy.

  ☐ Yes ☐ No  This applies to me.
  Here are some details about how it applies to me:

  _____

  _____

  _____

  _____

  _____


  Here are two small ways I can move forward successfully:

  _____

  _____

  _____

  _____

  _____

# How Can I Begin to Change?

*"Delay is the deadliest form of denial."*

—C. Northcote Parkinson

- **Make Notes**
  Make yourself visual reminders of the work you have to do. Putting a white board or corkboard next to the door allows for important reminders to read before you leave.

  ☐ Yes  ☐ No  This applies to me.
  Here are some details about how it applies to me:

  _____

  _____

  _____

  _____

  _____

  Here are two small ways I can move forward successfully:

  _____

  _____

  _____

  _____

  _____

# How Can I Begin to Change?

*"Even if you're on the right track, you'll get run over if you just sit there."*
—Will Rogers

- **Imagine a "Procrastination-Free" You**

  Imagine for a day that you are a well-organized, non-procrastinating person. How would you think and behave? Now bring those feelings and abilities into your real world.

  ☐ Yes   ☐ No  This applies to me.
  Here are some details about how it applies to me:

  _____

  _____

  _____

  _____

  _____

  Here are two small ways I can move forward successfully:

  _____

  _____

  _____

  _____

  _____

# How Can I Begin to Change?

*"What may be done at any time will be done at no time."*
—*Scottish Proverb*

- **Write Out a Plan for Yourself**

    Make yourself a daily schedule. If you're a "night person," make your plan the night before. If you're a "morning person" make your plan first thing upon awakening.

    ☐ Yes  ☐ No  This applies to me.
    Here are some details about how it applies to me:

    _____

    _____

    _____

    _____

    _____

    Here are two small ways I can move forward successfully:

    _____

    _____

    _____

    _____

    _____

# How Can I Begin to Change?

*"It's a job that's never started that takes the longest to finish."*

—*J. R. R. Tolkien*

- **Take Action Daily—No Matter How Small**

  Agree to start a project and stay with it for five minutes. Consider another five minutes at the end of the first.

  ☐ Yes   ☐ No  This applies to me.
  Here are some details about how it applies to me:

  _____

  _____

  _____

  _____

  _____

  Here are two small ways I can move forward successfully:

  _____

  _____

  _____

  _____

  _____

# How Can I Begin to Change?

*"The greatest amount of wasted time is the time not getting started."*
—Dawson Trotman

---

- **Worst Things First**

  Analyze your tasks from most unpleasant to most pleasant. Now here is the hard part; do the most unpleasant things first. Similar to riding a roller coaster, once you have gone over the scariest hill the rest is a piece of cake.

  ☐ Yes   ☐ No  This applies to me.
  Here are some details about how it applies to me:

  _____

  _____

  _____

  _____

  _____

  Here are two small ways I can move forward successfully:

  _____

  _____

  _____

  _____

# How Can I Begin to Change?

- **Make a List and Check It (More than) Twice**

  Make a daily list of tasks to be completed. Put about six items on a daily "to do" list and check them off as you complete each one. Being able to cross a task off often inspires us to do another. Prioritize the tasks. Make the list reasonable, but be specific.

  ☐ Yes   ☐ No  This applies to me.
  Here are some details about how it applies to me:

  _____

  _____

  _____

  _____

  _____

  Here are two small ways I can move forward successfully:

  _____

  _____

  _____

  _____

  _____

# How Can I Begin to Change

*"Do or do not do. There is no try."*

—Master Yoda

- **Schedule Time for Fun**

  When you are making your "to do" list, be sure to include fun activities. Scheduling fun activities provides the motivation to finish the other tasks more quickly.

  ☐ Yes ☐ No This applies to me.

  Here are some details about how it applies to me:

  _____

  _____

  _____

  _____

  _____

  Here are two small ways I can move forward successfully:

  _____

  _____

  _____

  _____

  _____

# How Can I Begin to Change?

*"To think too long about doing a thing often becomes its undoing."*

—Eva Young

## Specific Project Organization

- **Know Your Deadlines**

  Understand how much time you have to get the project done. Set your deadlines ahead of the actual drop-dead date to complete the project.

  ☐ Yes   ☐ No  This applies to me.
  Here are some details about how it applies to me:

  _____

  _____

  _____

  _____

  _____

  Here are two small ways I can move forward successfully:

  _____

  _____

  _____

  _____

  _____

# How Can I Begin to Change?

*"Nothing so perilous as procrastination."*

—John Lyly

- **Analyze the Project**

  Proper planning is important for optimum performance. Before jumping in, ask yourself pertinent questions about your task. Define the five to seven steps required for you to complete the task. The more planning you do before the task, the less time it is likely to take.

  ☐ Yes ☐ No This applies to me.
  Here are some details about how it applies to me:

  _____

  _____

  _____

  _____

  _____

  Here are two small ways I can move forward successfully:

  _____

  _____

  _____

  _____

  _____

# How Can I Begin to Change?

*"In the conduct of almost every affair slowness and procrastination are hateful."*

—Mark Anthony

- **Start Early**

  You most likely have a history of procrastination, otherwise you would not be reading this workbook. Recognize your procrastination and make it part of your work schedule. By starting the project early and adding the procrastination time, you will finish on time.

  ☐ Yes   ☐ No  This applies to me.

  Here are some details about how it applies to me:

  _____

  _____

  _____

  _____

  _____

  Here are two small ways I can move forward successfully:

  _____

  _____

  _____

  _____

  _____

# How Can I Begin to Change?

*"It is not because things are difficult that we do not dare, it is because we do not dare that they are difficult."*

—Seneca

- **Slice the Project into Smaller, More Manageable Pieces**
  A project doesn't have to be done at once. Start with a piece of the task so simple that you cannot possibly justify not doing it. Break down tasks into smaller, manageable steps. Large tasks may become overwhelming. Take one step at a time and don't worry about reaching the ultimate goal. Make use of small chunks of time.

  ☐ Yes   ☐ No  This applies to me.
  Here are some details about how it applies to me:

  _____

  _____

  _____

  _____

  _____

  Here are two small ways I can move forward successfully:

  _____

  _____

  _____

  _____

  _____

# How Can I Begin to Change?

*"He who has begun has half done. Dare to be wise; begin."*

—Horace

- **Get the Ball Rolling**

  Inertia is a wonderful thing! Once the ball starts moving, it continues to move until something stops it. Set a timer for fifteen minutes and take one small step to get started, like reading the first couple pages of the book you need to read. The important thing is to start.

  ☐ Yes   ☐ No  This applies to me.

  Here are some details about how it applies to me:

  _____

  _____

  _____

  _____

  _____

  Here are two small ways I can move forward successfully:

  _____

  _____

  _____

  _____

# How Can I Begin to Change?

*"You don't have to see the whole staircase, just take the first step."*
—Martin Luther King Jr.

- **Use Your Imagination**

  If you've got something hard to do, step outside, head to the park, sit by the pool—get out of your regular environment and think about the project ahead of time using your imagination or talking it over with a friend. Creative planning in your head, prior to beginning, will help you get started.

  ☐ Yes ☐ No This applies to me.
  Here are some details about how it applies to me:

  _____

  _____

  _____

  _____

  _____

  Here are two small ways I can move forward successfully:

  _____

  _____

  _____

  _____

  _____

# How Can I Begin to Change?

*"Procrastination is the art of keeping up with yesterday."*

—Don Marquis

- **Learn What You Need to Get the Job Done**

  If you don't know how to complete the task, ask someone. Literally allow yourself to admit to another, "I don't know how, but I am willing and want to learn." A little research beforehand will help you along the way.

  ☐ Yes ☐ No  This applies to me.

  Here are some details about how it applies to me:

  _____

  _____

  _____

  _____

  _____

  Here are two small ways I can move forward successfully:

  _____

  _____

  _____

  _____

  _____

# How Can I Begin to Change?

*"One of the greatest labor-saving inventions of today is tomorrow."*
—Vincent T. Foss

- **Use Your Impulsiveness**
  When you get going, keep going. Don't stop! Take action when you think of an idea, don't analyze it.

  ☐ Yes  ☐ No  This applies to me.
  Here are some details about how it applies to me:

  _____

  _____

  _____

  _____

  _____

  Here are two small ways I can move forward successfully:

  _____

  _____

  _____

  _____

# How Can I Begin to Change?

*"Don't wait for extraordinary circumstance to do good; try to use ordinary situations."*

—Charles Richter

## Create a Support System

- **Record Your Thoughts**
  Keep a journal (just one or two sentences will do) of how you are feeling and what you are thinking when delaying important tasks. Reviewing your journal can help you to identify patterns.

  ☐ Yes   ☐ No  This applies to me.
  Here are some details about how it applies to me:

  _____

  _____

  _____

  _____

  _____

  Here are two small ways I can move forward successfully:

  _____

  _____

  _____

  _____

# How Can I Begin to Change?

*"I love deadlines. I like the whooshing sound they make as they fly by."*
—Douglas Adams

- **Set Up a Buddy System**

  There is nothing like friends who can help us through life's tough times. The same is true for completing tasks you need to complete. Talk the project over with friends and ask them to check in on you on designated days to see how it is going. You will be motivated to work on the task because you are likely to want to report in with positive progress. You can do the same for them. You will have gone from a procrastinator to a coach, which feeds your own self-esteem—and higher self-esteem equals less procrastination.

  ☐ Yes   ☐ No  This applies to me.
  Here are some details about how it applies to me:

  _____

  _____

  _____

  _____

  _____

  Here are two small ways I can move forward successfully:

  _____

  _____

  _____

  _____

  _____

# How Can I Begin to Change?

*"Tomorrow is often the busiest day of the week."*

—Anonymous

- **Try to Gain Some Perspective**

  Change your language from "I have to" to "I get to." It isn't that large a leap if you understand the long-term goal. It is as simple as, "I have to go to the dentist." to "I get to finally deal with this tooth that has been bothering me." Self coaching can really change your outlook.

  ☐ Yes ☐ No This applies to me.

  Here are some details about how it applies to me:

  _____

  _____

  _____

  _____

  _____

  Here are two small ways I can move forward successfully:

  _____

  _____

  _____

  _____

  _____

# How Can I Begin to Change?

*"Anyone can do any amount of work providing it isn't the work he is supposed to be doing at that moment."*

—Robert Benchley

## Take Care of Yourself

- **Reward Yourself for the Completion of Tasks and Not Procrastinating**
  Play the carrot and stick game (except lose the stick) with yourself. Say to yourself, "When I finish these two chapters, I'm going to get a bite to eat with friends." Conversely you could say, "In order to get a bite to eat with my friends, I have to read these two chapters."

  ☐ Yes ☐ No This applies to me.
  Here are some details about how it applies to me:

  _____

  _____

  _____

  _____

  _____

  Here are two small ways I can move forward successfully:

  _____

  _____

  _____

  _____

  _____

# How Can I Begin to Change?

*"Procrastination: a hardening of the oughteries."*

**—Anonymous**

- **When Rewarding Yourself Don't Make the Reward Too Time-Consuming**
  You wouldn't want to write a paragraph in a report and then go off with your friends. Make sure there is an appropriate balance between the work and reward. Remember, you want to get the project done on time. Making the rewards too time-consuming is actually another form of procrastination.

  ☐ Yes  ☐ No  This applies to me.
  Here are some details about how it applies to me:

  _____

  _____

  _____

  _____

  _____

  Here are two small ways I can move forward successfully:

  _____

  _____

  _____

  _____

  _____

# How Can I Begin to Change?

*"Procrastination is the thief of time."*

—Edward Young

- **List the Pros and Cons of Procrastinating**

   It is important to know why procrastination is a problem and how procrastinating derails you. Jot down a few thoughts on how procrastinating on a particular project will hurt you and how starting the project will help. Try to be as specific as possible. The results will surprise you.

   ☐ Yes  ☐ No  This applies to me.

   Here are some details about how it applies to me:

   _____

   _____

   _____

   _____

   _____

   Here are two small ways I can move forward successfully:

   _____

   _____

   _____

   _____

   _____

# How Can I Begin to Change?

- **Stop Threatening Yourself**

  Here is where the vicious cycle begins. We procrastinate, and then punish ourselves for doing so. Next, we avoid those feelings by treating ourselves to a massage, a dough-nut, or new gadget to make ourselves feel better. In our subconscious, we know we really didn't deserve the treat, we then experience defeat and avoid the project at hand again. Avoid threatening or punishing yourself—take care of yourself instead.

  ☐ Yes  ☐ No  This applies to me.
  Here are some details about how it applies to me:

  _____

  _____

  _____

  _____

  _____


  Here are two small ways I can move forward successfully:

  _____

  _____

  _____

  _____

  _____

# How Can I Begin to Change?

*"Procrastination is the art of keeping up with yesterday and avoiding today."*
—Wayne Dyer

- **Envision Completion**

  Imagine what you will be able to do with your time when you don't have to work on the project. Imagine your feeling of accomplishment and joy at completing the task.

  ☐ Yes ☐ No This applies to me.
  Here are some details about how it applies to me:

  _____

  _____

  _____

  _____

  _____

  Here are two small ways I can move forward successfully:

  _____

  _____

  _____

  _____

  _____

- **Be Sure the Rest of Your Life Is in Good Shape**

  That feeling of being overwhelmed in other parts of our lives can cause avoidance of other "to dos" in addition to the project at hand. Capture your "to dos" in all areas of your life and put them on paper. Removing the brain-clutter clears the desk for project completion.

  ☐ Yes  ☐ No  This applies to me.

  Here are some details about how it applies to me:

  _____

  _____

  _____

  _____

  _____

  Here are two small ways I can move forward successfully:

  _____

  _____

  _____

  _____

# How Can I Begin to Change?

*"Procrastination gives you something to look forward to."*

—Joan Konner

- **Rage Against the Machine**

    If having to read four extremely boring chapters makes you angry, externalizing your feelings can be very helpful. Blow off some steam and then read the chapters.

    ☐ Yes    ☐ No  This applies to me.
    Here are some details about how it applies to me:

    _____

    _____

    _____

    _____

    _____

    Here are two small ways I can move forward successfully:

    _____

    _____

    _____

    _____

    _____

# How Can I Begin to Change?

*"I'm going to stop putting things off, starting tomorrow!"*

—Sam Levenson

- **Don't Expect Miracles**

  You didn't become a procrastinator overnight and you aren't going to erase it overnight either. Notice, as you practice your new anti-procrastination techniques, how you are improving. Little by little you will limit your old habits. There may be times when you slip a little. Notice the slip, understand and move forward.

  ☐ Yes ☐ No This applies to me.

  Here are some details about how it applies to me:

  _____

  _____

  _____

  _____

  _____

  Here are two small ways I can move forward successfully:

  _____

  _____

  _____

  _____

  _____

# How Can I Begin to Change?

*"I like work: it fascinates me. I can sit and look at it for hours."*

—Jerome K. Jerome

- **Know When You Are "Cheating"**

  Nobody knows you like you do. You know how you cheat, or how you justify your procrastination habit. Be aware of it and "come clean." Tell the truth to yourself.

  ☐ Yes  ☐ No  This applies to me.

  Here are some details about how it applies to me:

  _____

  _____

  _____

  _____

  _____

  Here are two small ways I can move forward successfully:

  _____

  _____

  _____

  _____

  _____

# How Can I Begin to Change?

*"Work expands so as to fill the time available for its completion."*
—C. Northcote Parkinson

- **Give Yourself Time to Change**
  Change is difficult. Focus on the areas of successful change, not on where you might be continuing to fail.

  ☐ Yes  ☐ No  This applies to me.
  Here are some details about how it applies to me:

  _____

  _____

  _____

  _____

  _____

  Here are two small ways I can move forward successfully:

  _____

  _____

  _____

  _____

  _____

# How Can I Begin to Change?

*"Tomorrow is the day when idlers work, and fools reform."*

—*Edward Young*

---

- **Expect and Forgive Backsliding**

   You are going to make mistakes and occasionally not live up to your own expectations. That's life. Forgive yourself and move on.

   ☐ Yes   ☐ No  This applies to me.
   Here are some details about how it applies to me:

   _____

   _____

   _____

   _____

   _____

   Here are two small ways I can move forward successfully:

   _____

   _____

   _____

   _____

   _____

# How Can I Begin to Change?

*"He who awaits much can expect little."*

—Gabriel García Márquez

- **Give Yourself Credit for Anything You Do**
  Changing long held habits is hard to do. Pat yourself on the back for your forward momentum.

  ☐ Yes   ☐ No  This applies to me.
  Here are some details about how it applies to me:

  _____

  _____

  _____

  _____

  _____

  Here are two small ways I can move forward successfully:

  _____

  _____

  _____

  _____

  _____

# How Can I Begin to Change?

*"One of these days is none of these days."*

—Henri Tubach and H. G. Bohn

- **Enjoy Your Freedom**

  When you complete an unpleasant task, take a moment to feel how nice it is to have it over and done with. No more nagging yourself to do the job, no more feeling like there's a weight on your shoulders. Celebrate.

  ☐ Yes ☐ No  This applies to me.
  Here are some details about how it applies to me:

  _____

  _____

  _____

  _____

  _____

  Here are two small ways I can move forward successfully:

  _____

  _____

  _____

  _____

## Care about yourself and forgive yourself a lot.

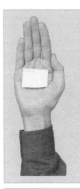

# Am I a Procrastinator?

*"A year from now you may wish you had started today."*

—Karen Lamb

In the previous sections we have defined procrastination, begun to see why it happens and found ways to change. Now it is time to determine in which areas of our lives we are most certain to procrastinate.

Read each question carefully to see how it may affect your life. Refer back to the previous sections for help if necessary. Although this section may look like a "test," it is not. It is a tool to help you understand yourself a little better.

As in the previous sections, there is space provided for you to react to the questions.

# Am I a Procrastinator?

*"Procrastination is the grave in which opportunity is buried."*

—**Anonymous**

## Personal Finance Procrastination

This section of the self-evaluation concentrates on financial tasks. The questions assume you are able to meet your financial commitments.

- **When your bills come in the mail, you (circle the answer that best applies to you):**
    1. Open them and pay them online that very day
    2. Open them and pay them via mail that very day
    3. Open them and pay all of your bills on a specified day during the month
    4. Leave them unopened until you pay them before the due date
    5. Pay them on the due date
    6. Pay them when memory serves
    7. Pay them late

    ☐ Yes   ☐ No   This is an issue for me.

    Because:

    _____

    _____

    _____

    _____

    _____

    Here is an idea how to change it:

    _____

    _____

    _____

    _____

    _____

# Am I a Procrastinator?

*"When there is a hill to climb, don't think that waiting will make it smaller."*
—**Anonymous**

- **Have you had to pay late fees on a statement(s) three times or more in the past two years?**

    ☐ Yes    ☐ No      This is an issue for me.

    Because:

    _____

    _____

    _____

    _____

    _____

    Here is an idea how to change it:

    _____

    _____

    _____

    _____

    _____

# Am I a Procrastinator?

*"Postpone not a good action."*

—Irish Proverb

- **Have you ever had a utility service cut off?**

  ☐ Yes   ☐ No   This is an issue for me.

  Because:

  _____

  _____

  _____

  _____

  _____


  Here is an idea how to change it:

  _____

  _____

  _____

  _____

  _____

# Am I a Procrastinator?

*"Anger is the only thing to put off till tomorrow."*

—Slovakian proverb

- **Has a collection agency called or written you regarding an overdue balance in the last two years?**

  ☐ Yes   ☐ No   This is an issue for me.

  Because:

  _____

  _____

  _____

  _____

  _____

  Here is an idea how to change it:

  _____

  _____

  _____

  _____

  _____

# Am I a Procrastinator?

*"Procrastination and worry are the twin thieves that will try to rob you of your brilliance—but even the smallest action will drive them from your camp."*

—Gil Atkinson

- **When your employer pays you, you (circle the answer that best applies to you):**
  1. Have automatic deposit
  2. Deposit the funds the same day
  3. Deposit the check on the same day each month
  4. Misplace the check on your work or home desk
  5. Carry the check around for weeks in your wallet

  ☐ Yes   ☐ No   This is an issue for me.

  Because:

  _____

  _____

  _____

  _____

  _____

  Here is an idea how to change it:

  _____

  _____

  _____

  _____

  _____

# Am I a Procrastinator?

*"Procrastination is the thief of time."*

—Edward Young

- **Have you ever needed to have a check rewritten to you because you didn't cash it in time?**

    ☐ Yes   ☐ No    This is an issue for me:

    Because:

    _____

    _____

    _____

    _____

    _____

    Here is an idea how to change it:

    _____

    _____

    _____

    _____

    _____

# Am I a Procrastinator?

*"Ah! The clock is always slow; it is later thank you think."*

—Robert W. Service

- **When your monthly bank statement arrives, you (circle the answer that best applies to you):**

  1. Balance the account on your computer within two or three days
  2. Balance the account by hand within two or three days
  3. Balance the account whichever way within the month
  4. Balance several months at one time
  5. Open the envelope to see the balance and put it into a drawer and not balance it
  6. Don't open the envelope

  ☐ Yes   ☐ No   This is an issue for me.

  Because:

  _____

  _____

  _____

  _____

  _____

  Here is an idea how to change it:

  _____

  _____

  _____

  _____

  _____

- **If the answer to the previous question is either answer "4," "5" or "6" how many months behind in balancing your account are you? (Circle the answer that best applies to you.)**

  1. One month
  2. One to four months behind
  3. Four to eight months behind
  4. Eight months to one year
  5. More than one year

☐ Yes    ☐ No     This is an issue for me.

Because:

_____

_____

_____

_____

_____

Here is an idea how to change it:

_____

_____

_____

_____

# Am I a Procrastinator?

*"Nothing is so exhausting as indecision, and nothing so futile."*
—Bertrand Russell

- **Have you checked to see the status of your credit report and credit rating?**

☐ Yes  ☐ No   This is an issue for me.

Because:

_____

_____

_____

_____

_____

Here is an idea how to change it:

_____

_____

_____

_____

_____

# Am I a Procrastinator?

*"He who puts off nothing till tomorrow has done a great deal."*

—Baltasar Graci

- **When your income tax forms come in the mail, you (circle the answer that best applies to you):**

1. Prepare the materials for your accountant or prepare the return yourself within one week
2. Prepare the materials for your accountant or prepare the return yourself within one month
3. Prepare the materials for your accountant or prepare the return yourself by April 1
4. Scramble at the last minute to gather the materials and get the return on time
5. Delay and ask for an extension and possibly pay late fees and penalties
6. Don't file your taxes

☐ Yes   ☐ No     This is an issue for me.

Because:

_____

_____

_____

_____

_____

Here is an idea how to change it:

_____

_____

_____

_____

_____

# Am I a Procrastinator?

*"He who postpones the hour of living is like the rustic who waits for the river to run out before he crosses."*

—Horace

- **If you have had the opportunity to apply for a loan for a home, car or school, you (circle the answer that best applies to you):**

    1.  Have not applied for a loan
    2.  Submitted the paper work ahead of time
    3.  Submitted the paper work by the deadline
    4.  Needed to ask for an extension
    5.  Failed to submit the paper work by the deadline and lost the loan

☐ Yes  ☐ No    This is an issue for me.

Because:

_____

_____

_____

_____

_____

Here is an idea how to change it:

_____

_____

_____

_____

_____

# Am I a Procrastinator?

*"The opportunity often slips away while we deliberate on it."*

—Syrus

- Using the financial questions as a guide, list two of the most crucial situations that confronted you:

_____

Situation #1

_____

Way in which you procrastinated

_____

Underlying reason for the procrastination

_____

What technique can you use to change for the future?




_____

Situation #2

_____

Way in which you procrastinated

_____

Underlying reason for the procrastination

_____

What technique can you use to change for the future?

# Am I a Procrastinator?

*"Only Robinson Crusoe had everything done by Friday."*

**—Unknown**

## Office Procrastination

This section of the self-evaluation concentrates on your activities at your work, whether you work from home or not.

- **The following best describes how you work with deadlines (circle the answer that best applies to you):**

  1. You complete a project far ahead of the deadline in case of problems
  2. You like the crunch of a deadline but still like to finish ahead just in case
  3. You're most efficient when you know the deadline is near
  4. You love racing against the clock to meet a deadline
  5. You don't care about deadlines, so you rarely meet them

  ☐ Yes    ☐ No     This is an issue for me.

  Because:

  _____

  _____

  _____

  _____

  _____

  Here is an idea how to change it:

  _____

  _____

  _____

  _____

  _____

# Am I a Procrastinator?

*"Every duty which is bidden to wait returns with seven fresh duties at its back."*

—Charles Kingsley

- **How do you set defined deadlines for yourself and others? (Circle the answer that best applies to you.)**

    1.  You evaluate the project with input from staff and build in extra time just in case
    2.  You see how similar projects were done and set similar deadlines
    3.  You set the deadline sooner than needed to energize yourself and staff
    4.  You let your staff tell you what the deadline should be
    5.  You don't set deadlines

    ☐ Yes   ☐ No   This is an issue for me.

    Because:

    _____

    _____

    _____

    _____

    _____

    Here is an idea how to change it:

    _____

    _____

    _____

    _____

    _____

# Am I a Procrastinator?

*"If it weren't for the last minute, I wouldn't get anything done."*

—Unknown

- **What would you say best describes how you meet your deadlines? (Circle the answer that best applies to you.)**

    1. You are always ahead of schedule
    2. You often meet your deadlines
    3. You meet your deadlines, but use overtime to get it done
    4. You like to redefine your deadlines as the job progresses
    5. For some reason you rarely meet your deadlines

    ☐ Yes  ☐ No   This is an issue for me.

    Because:

    _____

    _____

    _____

    _____

    Here is an idea how to change it:

    _____

    _____

    _____

    _____

    _____

# Am I a Procrastinator?

*"Procrastination . . . is the thief of our self respect. It nags us and spoils our fun. It deprives us of the fullest realization of our ambitions and hopes."*
—Thomas S. Monson

- **On those occasions when you fail to meet deadlines, what would you say are the main reasons? (Circle the answer that best applies to you.)**

    1.  You didn't take into consideration all of the variables of the project
    2.  You got a late start on the project
    3.  Other projects got in the way
    4.  Outside events slowed you down
    5.  You didn't enforce the deadline

    ☐ Yes  ☐ No     This is an issue for me.

    Because:

    _____

    _____

    _____

    _____

    _____

    Here is an idea how to change it:

    _____

    _____

    _____

    _____

    _____

# Am I a Procrastinator?

*"Waiting is a trap. There will always be reasons to wait. . . . The truth is, there are only two things in life, reasons and results, and reasons simply don't count."*

—Robert Anthony

- **Would you say that your day consists of (circle the answer that best applies to you):**

1. Dealing with a list of tasks you have decided on
2. Prioritizing a group's tasks
3. A lot of meetings
4. Dealing with a constant flow of e-mails and phone calls
5. Shuffling papers
6. Putting out fires

☐ Yes ☐ No This is an issue for me.

Because:

_____

_____

_____

_____

_____

Here is an idea how to change it:

_____

_____

_____

_____

_____

# Am I a Procrastinator?

*"Twenty years from now, you will be more disappointed by things that you didn't do than by the things that you did do."*

—Mark Twain

- **When you start work in the morning, you (circle the answer that best applies to you):**

    1. Take a few minutes to review what needs to be done based on your plan
    2. Pick up the first thing you see on your desk and work on it
    3. Do tasks that you enjoy
    4. Do the most important task
    5. See what the day brings you
    6. Chat with colleagues and focus on non-work related e-mails

    ☐ Yes   ☐ No     This is an issue for me.

    Because:

    _____

    _____

    _____

    _____

    _____

    Here is an idea how to change it:

    _____

    _____

    _____

    _____

    _____

# Am I a Procrastinator?

*"Someday is not a day of the week."*

—Unknown

- **How often are employees, vendors or clients waiting for you to complete tasks so they can do their work? (Circle the answer that best applies to you.)**

    1.  Always
    2.  Sometimes
    3.  Rarely
    4.  Never
    5.  This doesn't apply to you

    ☐ Yes    ☐ No    This is an issue for me.

    Because:

    _____

    _____

    _____

    _____

    _____

    Here is an idea how to change it:

    _____

    _____

    _____

    _____

    _____

# Am I a Procrastinator?

*"The past does not equal the future unless you live there."*
—Anthony Robbins

- **How would you characterize the level of respect you get from your coworkers or employees? (Circle the answer that best applies to you.)**

    1. Very high
    2. High
    3. Neutral
    4. Poor
    5. Very poor

    ☐ Yes   ☐ No   This is an issue for me.

    Because:

    _____

    _____

    _____

    _____

    _____

    Here is an idea how to change it:

    _____

    _____

    _____

    _____

    _____

# Am I a Procrastinator?

*"There's nothing to match curling up with a good book when there's a repair job to be done around the house."*

—Joe Ryan

- **When a new document comes into your possession, you (circle the answer that best applies to you):**

    1. Quickly evaluate it to act on, file it or throw it away
    2. Leave it on your desk to read later
    3. Leave on your desk to file later
    4. Read it and leave it on your desk
    5. Get to it when you can

    ☐ Yes    ☐ No    This is an issue for me.

    Because:

    _____

    _____

    _____

    _____

    _____

    Here is an idea how to change it:

    _____

    _____

    _____

    _____

    _____

# Am I a Procrastinator?

*"Procrastination is suicide on the installment plan."*

—Anonymous

- **When you need a document from your desk while you are away from the office, how would you describe the effort for others to find it for you? (Circle the answer that best applies to you.)**

    1. Most often they could find it with simple directions
    2. If you remember where it is you might be able to tell them
    3. Your office is cluttered, so it might take them a while
    4. You'd be afraid that they would have to dig through something they shouldn't see
    5. You wouldn't be able to begin to tell them

    ☐ Yes    ☐ No    This is an issue for me.

    Because:

    _____

    _____

    _____

    _____

    _____

    Here is an idea how to change it:

    _____

    _____

    _____

    _____

    _____

# Am I a Procrastinator?

*"If you can dream it, you can do it. Always remember, this whole thing was started by a mouse."*

—Walt Disney

- **When a good friend calls during business hours, (circle the answer that best applies to you):**

    1. You chat briefly to assess if it is an emergency, if not, excuse yourself to get back to work
    2. You talk for about five minutes; just long enough to be friendly
    3. You talk for about ten minutes; friends know it's okay to call you at work
    4. If you're not into what you're doing, you'll talk for a while
    5. You believe that work is just work, but friendship lasts

    ☐ Yes  ☐ No    This is an issue for me.

    Because:

    _____

    _____

    _____

    _____

    _____

    Here is an idea how to change it:

    _____

    _____

    _____

    _____

# Am I a Procrastinator?

*"You can't get much done by starting tomorrow."*

—Unknown

- **When you go to a meeting outside your office, (circle the answer that best applies to you):**

    1. You always prepare ahead of time and arrive on time
    2. You sometimes forget you have a meeting or where it is and scramble to get there
    3. You have a hard time getting out of the office; something always comes up
    4. You seem to always cut it close, even though you're not often late
    5. People plan on you being late, it's what you're known for

    ☐ Yes  ☐ No     This is an issue for me.

    Because:

    _____

    _____

    _____

    _____

    _____

    Here is an idea how to change it:

    _____

    _____

    _____

    _____

    _____

# Am I a Procrastinator?

*"You cannot win if you do not begin."*

—Unknown

---

- **How would you assess the separation between your work life and your home life? (Circle the answer that best applies to you.)**

  1. Work is work and home is home, you very rarely mix the two.
  2. Pretty good separation, but sometimes you have to make compromises
  3. Your family is everything to you; work is a far second
  4. You're a workaholic, your family has gotten used to it
  5. You've never really thought about it

  ☐ Yes    ☐ No    This is an issue for me.

  Because:

  _____

  _____

  _____

  _____

  _____

  Here is an idea how to change it:

  _____

  _____

  _____

  _____

  _____

# READER/CUSTOMER CARE SURVEY

We care about your opinions! Please take a moment to fill out our online Reader Survey at **http://survey.hcibooks.com.**
As a **"THANK YOU"** you will receive a **VALUABLE INSTANT COUPON** towards future book purchases as well as a **SPECIAL GIFT** available
only online! Or, you may mail this card back to us and we will send you a copy of our exciting catalog with your valuable coupon inside.
(PLEASE PRINT IN ALL CAPS)

First Name _____ MI. _____ Last Name _____

Address _____ City _____

State _____ Zip _____ Email _____

**1. Gender**
- ❏ Female ❏ Male

**2. Age**
- ❏ 8 or younger
- ❏ 9-12 ❏ 13-16
- ❏ 17-20 ❏ 21-30
- ❏ 31+

**3. Did you receive this book as a gift?**
- ❏ Yes ❏ No

**4. Annual Household Income**
- ❏ under $25,000
- ❏ $25,000 - $34,999
- ❏ $35,000 - $49,999
- ❏ $50,000 - $74,999
- ❏ over $75,000

**5. What are the ages of the children living in your house?**
- ❏ 0 - 14 ❏ 15+

**6. Marital Status**
- ❏ Single
- ❏ Married
- ❏ Divorced
- ❏ Widowed

**7. How did you find out about the book?**
*(please choose one)*
- ❏ Recommendation
- ❏ Store Display
- ❏ Online
- ❏ Catalog/Mailing
- ❏ Interview/Review

**8. Where do you usually buy books?**
*(please choose one)*
- ❏ Bookstore
- ❏ Online
- ❏ Book Club/Mail Order
- ❏ Price Club (Sam's Club, Costco's, etc.)
- ❏ Retail Store (Target, Wal-Mart, etc.)

**9. What subject do you enjoy reading about the most?**
*(please choose one)*
- ❏ Parenting/Family
- ❏ Relationships
- ❏ Recovery/Addictions
- ❏ Health/Nutrition
- ❏ Christianity
- ❏ Spirituality/Inspiration
- ❏ Business Self-help
- ❏ Women's Issues
- ❏ Sports

**10. What attracts you most to a book?**
*(please choose one)*
- ❏ Title
- ❏ Cover Design
- ❏ Author
- ❏ Content

TAPE IN MIDDLE; DO NOT STAPLE

# BUSINESS REPLY MAIL
FIRST-CLASS MAIL  PERMIT NO 45  DEERFIELD BEACH, FL

POSTAGE WILL BE PAID BY ADDRESSEE

Health Communications, Inc.
3201 SW 15th Street
Deerfield Beach FL 33442-9875

FOLD HERE

**Comments**

# Am I a Procrastinator?

*"Vagueness and procrastination are ever a comfort to the frail in spirit."*
—John Updike

- **How would you describe yourself at work? (Circle the answer that best applies to you.)**

   1. Friendly, calm and confident
   2. Slightly behind but always catching up
   3. Happy until something throws you for a loop
   4. Under pressure in crisis mode
   5. Waiting for the next shoe to drop

   ☐ Yes   ☐ No    This is an issue for me.

   Because:

   _____

   _____

   _____

   _____

   _____

   Here is an idea how to change it:

   _____

   _____

   _____

   _____

# Am I a Procrastinator?

*"Delay and procrastination is hateful."*

—Cicero

- **Do you look for excuses to avoid work that you feel you are not good at?**

    ☐ Yes    ☐ No     This is an issue for me.

    Because:

    _____

    _____

    _____

    _____

    _____

    Here is an idea how to change it:

    _____

    _____

    _____

    _____

    _____

# Am I a Procrastinator?

*"Puttine off an easy thing makes it hard. Putting off a hard thing makes it impossible."*

—George H. Lorimer

- **Using the office procrastination questions as a guide, list two of the most crucial situations that confronted you:**

_____

Situation #1

_____

Way in which you procrastinated

_____

Underlying reason for the procrastination

_____

What technique can you use to change for the future?




_____

Situation #2

_____

Way in which you procrastinated

_____

Underlying reason for the procrastination

_____

What technique can you use to change for the future?

# Am I a Procrastinator?

*"By the streets of 'by and by' one arrives at the house of 'never.'"*
—Miguel de Cervantes

## Relationship Procrastination

This section of the self-evaluation concentrates on your activities in your interpersonal relationships.

- **What do you think your friends and family would say about you and procrastination? (Circle the answer that best applies to you.)**

  1. You procrastinate a little, everyone does, but it's not a big deal
  2. You're such a great person, they just wish you could get your life together a little bit more
  3. They just wish you could be more dependable
  4. They find it irritating to be around you, they're so organized compared to you
  5. They can't be around you; your inability to deal with life drives them crazy

  ☐ Yes  ☐ No    This is an issue for me.

  Because:

  _____

  _____

  _____

  _____

  _____

  Here is an idea how to change it:

  _____

  _____

  _____

  _____

  _____

# Am I a Procrastinator?

*"By one delay after another they spin out their whole lives, till there's no more future left for them."*

—L'Estrange

- **You get home from an evening out and you check your messages and find several calls from family and friends; you (circle the answer that best applies to you):**

  1. Phone them all back as soon as you can
  2. Save the messages, settle in and then call each one back
  3. Save the messages, settle in and call only the ones you really care about that night and save the rest for another time
  4. Save the messages, do the work you promised yourself you would complete and then call them back when you get the chance
  5. Forget to call them back

  ☐ Yes　☐ No　　　This is an issue for me.

  Because:

  _____

  _____

  _____

  _____

  _____

  Here is an idea how to change it:

  _____

  _____

  _____

  _____

  _____

# Am I a Procrastinator?

*"For yesterday was once tomorrow."*

—Persius

- **You are in a romantic relationship that is just not working out for you and you decide to end it, so you (circle the answer that best applies to you):**

1. Talk to him or her as soon as you can
2. Think about it for a week before talking about it
3. Think about it for a month before talking about it
4. Try and talk yourself out of ending the relationship
5. Send an e-mail or leave an answering machine message ending the relationship
6. Let it drag on and hope he or she breaks up with you
7. Disappear without contacting the other person

☐ Yes   ☐ No     This is an issue for me.

Because:

_____

_____

_____

_____

_____

Here is an idea how to change it:

_____

_____

_____

_____

_____

# Am I a Procrastinator?

*"Indulge in procrastination, and in time you will come to this, that because a thing ought to be done, therefore you can't do it."*

—Charles Buxton

- **You arrange to go out with a friend for a movie; during the evening he or she says that you should go to a movie that you don't want to see, so you (circle the answer that best applies to you):**

    1. Immediately tell him or her that you don't want to go to that movie
    2. Wait until you get to the theater before telling him
    3. Drag your feet so you miss the movie
    4. Go to the movie in a sour mood
    5. Make an agreement to endure this movie and next time you get to select the movie or activity

    ☐ Yes　　☐ No　　This is an issue for me.

    Because:

    _____

    _____

    _____

    _____

    _____

    Here is an idea how to change it:

    _____

    _____

    _____

    _____

# Am I a Procrastinator?

*"He who hestitates is a damned fool."*

—Mae West

- **An old friend sent you a birthday gift and now it is a month past your birthday, you (circle the answer that best applies to you):**
    1. Immediately call and thank your friend for the gift and apologize for not calling sooner
    2. Call in about a week and thank him or her for the gift
    3. Call and pretend you didn't get the gift
    4. Call when you know he or she won't be home
    5. Don't call and risk he or she feeling hurt or wondering if you are okay

    ☐ Yes   ☐ No    This is an issue for me.

    Because:

    _____

    _____

    _____

    _____

    _____

    Here is an idea how to change it:

    _____

    _____

    _____

    _____

    _____

# Am I a Procrastinator?

*"All things come to those who wait, but when they come they're out of date."*
—Unknown

- **When it is your turn to pick up a friend for an outing, you are most often (circle the answer that best applies to you):**

1. Right on time
2. Five to ten minutes late
3. Ten to fifteen minutes late
4. Around twenty minutes late
5. Your friends seem to always volunteer to pick you up

☐ Yes   ☐ No      This is an issue for me.

Because:

_____

_____

_____

_____

_____

Here is an idea how to change it:

_____

_____

_____

_____

_____

# Am I a Procrastinator?

*"The butterfly counts not months but moments, and has time enough."*
—Rabindranath Tagore

- **You volunteer to take pictures at your friend's wedding; you (circle the answer that best applies to you):**

  1. Develop the photos immediately
  2. Develop them within the month
  3. Develop them within the year
  4. Not develop them, but always promise you will
  5. Lose the file or photos

  ☐ Yes  ☐ No   This is an issue for me.

  Because:

  _____

  _____

  _____

  _____

  _____

  Here is an idea how to change it:

  _____

  _____

  _____

  _____

# Am I a Procrastinator?

*"No age or time of life, no position or circumstance, has a monopoly on success. Any age is the right age to start doing!"*

—Ralph Gerard

- **Using the relationship procrastination questions as a guide, list two of the most crucial situations that confronted you:**

Situation #1

Way in which you procrastinated

Underlying reason for the procrastination

What technique can you use to change for the future?

Situation #2

Way in which you procrastinated

Underlying reason for the procrastination

What technique can you use to change for the future?

# Am I a Procrastinator?

*"A wise person does at once, what a fool does at last. Both do the same thing; only at different times."*

—Lord Acton

## Traveling Procrastination

This section of the self-evaluation concentrates on your activities during your travels.

- **You have to go out of town on a business trip in five weeks, do you (circle the answer that best applies to you):**

   1. Make your plane reservation now to save as much money as you can
   2. Make your plane reservation two weeks out to get a smaller discount
   3. Make the reservation one week out to hopefully still get a small discount
   4. Pay full fare
   5. Go to the airport and try to get a cheaper fare by flying stand by

   ☐ Yes   ☐ No   This is an issue for me.

   Because:

   _____

   _____

   _____

   _____

   _____

   Here is an idea how to change it:

   _____

   _____

   _____

   _____

   _____

# Am I a Procrastinator?

*"He who waits upon fortune is never sure of dinner."*

—Benjamin Franklin

- You and some friends are flying out of town for a trip that you have been looking forward to for some time. It is the morning of the trip and when they come to pick you up, you are (circle the answer that best applies to you):

1.    Ready to go with bags packed and ticket in hand
2.    Bags packed but can't find your ticket
3.    Still packing your bags, assuring them that everything is going to be okay
4.    Starting to get ready to pack
5.    Overslept
6.    Not ready and tell them to go on ahead and you will meet them

☐ Yes    ☐ No        This is an issue for me.

Because:

_____

_____

_____

_____

_____

Here is an idea how to change it:

_____

_____

_____

_____

_____

# Am I a Procrastinator?

*"He who begins and does not finish loves their pains."*

—Proverb

- **It is your day to plan your four friends' activities while on your vacation in Hawaii, you (circle the answer that best applies to you):**

  1. Have a hard time deciding and leave it up to them
  2. Choose three options for your friends to vote on
  3. Pick something that you have wanted to do
  4. Forget to do it
  5. Pick something that you and your friends will want to do
  6. Have it selected before you even arrive in Hawaii

  ☐ Yes  ☐ No    This is an issue for me.

  Because:

  _____

  _____

  _____

  _____

  _____

  Here is an idea how to change it:

  _____

  _____

  _____

  _____

# Am I a Procrastinator?

*"Don't put off till tomorrow what can be enjoyed today."*

—Josh Billings

- **Which statement best demonstrates your demeanor on a pleasure trip? (Circle the answer that best applies to you.)**

    1. Calmly enjoying your time
    2. Busy deciding what to do next
    3. Concerned about work not done back home
    4. Running late from event to event
    5. Didn't get around to making plane reservations

    ☐ Yes  ☐ No    This is an issue for me.

    Because:

    _____

    _____

    _____

    _____

    _____

    Here is an idea how to change it:

    _____

    _____

    _____

    _____

    _____

# Am I a Procrastinator?

*"If you want to make an easy job seem mighty hard, just keep putting off doing it."*

—Olin Miller

- **Using the traveling procrastination questions as a guide, list two of the most crucial situations that confronted you:**

_____

Situation #1

_____

Way in which you procrastinated

_____

Underlying reason for the procrastination

_____

What technique can you use to change for the future?




_____

Situation #2

_____

Way in which you procrastinated

_____

Underlying reason for the procrastination

_____

What technique can you use to change for the future?

# Am I a Procrastinator?

*"I wasted time, and now doth time waste me."*

—**William Shakespeare**

## Living Area Procrastination

This section of the self-evaluation concentrates on your living area.

- **What statement best describes your living area? (Circle the answer that best applies to you.)**

  1. Very neat and tidy
  2. Few papers lying around but other than that fine
  3. Happily cluttered
  4. Very messy
  5. Filthy—you don't invite others over for fear of embarrassment

  ☐ Yes   ☐ No      This is an issue for me.

  Because:

  _____

  _____

  _____

  _____

  _____

  Here is an idea how to change it:

  _____

  _____

  _____

  _____

  _____

# Am I a Procrastinator?

*"Defer no time, delays have dangerous ends."*

—William Shakespeare

- **How would you say your friends or family describe your living area? (Circle the answer that best applies to you.)**

  1. Clean
  2. Cluttered
  3. Messy
  4. It is very difficult to be around.
  5. You don't invite your friends over

  ☐ Yes   ☐ No      This is an issue for me.

  Because:

  _____

  _____

  _____

  _____

  _____

  Here is an idea how to change it:

  _____

  _____

  _____

  _____

# Am I a Procrastinator?

*" . . . if we wait for the moment when everything, absolutely everything is ready, we shall never begin."*

—Ivan Turgenev

- **Which statement best describes your thoughts about your living area? (Circle the answer that best applies to you.)**

    1. You have too much stuff
    2. You're too disorganized
    3. You can't seem to part with anything
    4. Your place has grown too small for the amount of possessions you have
    5. You're immobilized by your living area

    ☐ Yes    ☐ No     This is an issue for me.

    Because:

    _____

    _____

    _____

    _____

    Here is an idea how to change it:

    _____

    _____

    _____

    _____

# Am I a Procrastinator?

*"Nothing was ever done so systematically as nothing is being done now."*
-Woodrow T. Wilson

- **Have you ever opened a kitchen cupboard and had its contents fall to the floor?**

☐ Yes ☐ No     This is an issue for me.

Because:

_____

_____

_____

_____

_____

Here is an idea how to change it:

_____

_____

_____

_____

_____

# Am I a Procrastinator?

*"There are two kinds of people, those who finish what they start and so on."*
—Robert Byrne

- **You don't own a dishwasher and you make a delicious dinner that uses four of your pots; you (circle the answer that best applies to you):**

1. Clean them as soon as you use them
2. Clean them after dinner
3. Clean them the next morning
4. Clean them the next time you need to use them

☐ Yes ☐ No     This is an issue for me.

Because:

_____

_____

_____

_____

Here is an idea how to change it:

_____

_____

_____

_____

# Am I a Procrastinator?

*"There is nothing so fatal to character as half finished tasks."*
—David Lloyd George

- **When you go out to the garage, are you able to find what you need?**

☐ Yes   ☐ No      This is an issue for me.

Because:

_____

_____

_____

_____

_____

Here is an idea how to change it:

_____

_____

_____

_____

_____

# Am I a Procrastinator?

*"The nature of men is always the same; it is their habits that separate them."*
—Confucius

- **After reading the daily paper, you (circle the answer that best applies to you):**

    1.  Throw it away immediately
    2.  Stack the papers to be thrown away in a few days
    3.  Leave the papers where you read them
    4.  Keep the papers for months

    ☐ Yes    ☐ No    This is an issue for me.

    Because:

    _____

    _____

    _____

    _____

    _____

    Here is an idea how to change it:

    _____

    _____

    _____

    _____

    _____

# Am I a Procrastinator?

*"I do my work at the same time each day—the last minute!"*

—Unknown

- **Which statement accurately reflects your thoughts regarding your living area? (Circle the answer that best applies to you.)**

  1. You are happy with it
  2. It sometimes gets to you
  3. You wish you knew where to start to clean it up
  4. You are depressed by your surroundings

  ☐ Yes   ☐ No      This is an issue for me.

  Because:

  _____

  _____

  _____

  _____

  Here is an idea how to change it:

  _____

  _____

  _____

  _____

# Am I a Procrastinator?

*"Do nothing by halves which can be done by quarters."*

—F. R. Scott

- **Please complete the sentence "I clean my desk or my dining room table . . . "
  (circle the answer that best applies to you):**

  1. Every day
  2. Once a week
  3. When it gets messy
  4. When I can't find something
  5. When my friends are coming over

  ☐ Yes    ☐ No    This is an issue for me.

  Because:

  _____

  _____

  _____

  _____

  _____

  Here is an idea how to change it:

  _____

  _____

  _____

  _____

  _____

# Am I a Procrastinator?

*"Neither a wise nor a brave man lies down on the tracks of history to wait for the train of the future to run over him."*

—Dwight D. Eisenhower

- **Using the living area procrastination questions as a guide, list two of the most crucial situations that confronted you:**

_____

Situation #1

_____

Way in which you procrastinated

_____

Underlying reason for the procrastination

_____

What technique can you use to change for the future?

_____

Situation #2

_____

Way in which you procrastinated

_____

Underlying reason for the procrastination

_____

What technique can you use to change for the future?

# Am I a Procrastinator?

*"If you procrastinate when faced with a big difficult problem . . . break the problem into parts, and handle one part at a time."*

—Robert Collier

## Medical Issues Procrastination

This section of the self-evaluation concentrates on your medical issues.

- **You have a strange pain in your stomach; it doesn't feel like anything you have felt before (circle the answer that best applies to you):**

    1. You immediately call the doctor for an appointment
    2. You wait a few days to see if it gets worse or it goes away
    3. You call the doctor in about a week
    4. Something always comes up and you never call the doctor
    5. You are afraid of doctors

    ☐ Yes   ☐ No        This is an issue for me.

    Because:

    _____

    _____

    _____

    _____

    _____

    Here is an idea how to change it:

    _____

    _____

    _____

    _____

    _____

# Am I a Procrastinator?

*The average American worker has fifty interruptions a day, of which seventy percent have nothing to do with work."*

—W. Edwards Deming

- **You have a medication that you must take each morning, you (circle the answer that best applies to you):**

  1. Set your pills out in advance for the week and take them each morning
  2. Take them at the same time each morning
  3. Sometimes take them late
  4. Take them when you remember
  5. Something always seems to come up and you most often forget to take them

  ☐ Yes      ☐ No      This is an issue for me.

  Because:

  _____

  _____

  _____

  _____

  Here is an idea how to change it:

  _____

  _____

  _____

  _____

# Am I a Procrastinator?

*"When a man does a household job, he goes through three periods: contemplating how it will be done; contemplating when it will be done; and contemplating."*

—Marcelene Cox

- **When was the last time you had a medical checkup not related to a specific issue? (Circle the answer that best applies to you.)**

    1. This past year
    2. Three years ago
    3. Five years ago
    4. Ten years ago
    5. You don't remember

    ☐ Yes   ☐ No      This is an issue for me.

    Because:

    _____

    _____

    _____

    _____

    _____

    Here is an idea how to change it:

    _____

    _____

    _____

    _____

    _____

# Am I a Procrastinator?

*"Seize the day, put no trust in tomorrow."*

—Unknown

- **Have you ever run out of a medication you need to take?**

☐ Yes   ☐ No      This is an issue for me.

Because:

_____

_____

_____

_____

_____

Here is an idea how to change it:

_____

_____

_____

_____

_____

# Am I a Procrastinator?

*"Procrastination is the bad habit of putting off until the day after tomorrow what should have been done the day before yesterday."*

—Napoleon Hill

- **Are you currently experiencing medical issues that you have not talked to a doctor about?**

☐ Yes     ☐ No     This is an issue for me.

Because:

_____

_____

_____

_____

_____

Here is an idea how to change it:

_____

_____

_____

_____

_____

# Am I a Procrastinator?

*"Nothing makes me more productive than the last minute."*

—**Unknown**

- **You've recently had a medical appointment and now must fill out insurance forms and send them in; you (circle the answer that best applies to you):**

  1. Immediately fill the forms out and send them in
  2. Set them aside to work on later
  3. Send them in within the month
  4. Send them in when you get a letter from the company
  5. Never send them in

  ☐ Yes   ☐ No        This is an issue for me.

  Because:

  _____

  _____

  _____

  _____

  _____

  Here is an idea how to change it:

  _____

  _____

  _____

  _____

  _____

# Am I a Procrastinator?

*"Perception is strong and sight weak. In strategy it is important to see distant things as if they were close and to take a distanced view of close things."*
—Miyamoto Musashi

- **Using the medical procrastination questions as a guide, list two of the most crucial situations that confronted you:**

_____

Situation #1

_____

Way in which you procrastinated

_____

Underlying reason for the procrastination

_____

What technique can you use to change for the future?



_____

Situation #2

_____

Way in which you procrastinated

_____

Underlying reason for the procrastination

_____

What technique can you use to change for the future?

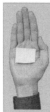

# Am I a Procrastinator?

*"Until you value yourself, you will not value your time. Until you value your time, you will not do anything with it."*

—M. Scott Peck

## Study Issues Procrastination

This section of the self-evaluation concentrates on your study issues.

- **You have a fifteen page paper on the history of automobiles due in three weeks, you (circle the answer that best applies to you):**

    1. Begin working right away on the project
    2. Start working in about a week
    3. Start in two weeks
    4. Start writing the night before
    5. Don't finish the paper

    ☐ Yes   ☐ No      This is an issue for me.

    Because:

    _____

    _____

    _____

    _____

    _____

    Here is an idea how to change it:

    _____

    _____

    _____

    _____

    _____

# Am I a Procrastinator?

*"During a very busy life I have often been asked, 'How did you manage to do it all?' The answer is very simple. It is because I did everything promptly."*
—*Richard Tangye*

- **Do you watch television or listen to music while you study, and which seems to distract you more? (Circle the answer that best applies to you.)**

   1. Television
   2. Music

   ☐ Yes  ☐ No  This is an issue for me.

   Because:

   _____

   _____

   _____

   _____

   _____

   Here is an idea how to change it:

   _____

   _____

   _____

   _____

   _____

# Am I a Procrastinator?

*"If once a man indulges himself in murder, very soon he comes to think little of robbing; and from robbing he comes next to drinking and sabbath-breaking, and from that to incivility and procrastination."*

—Thomas de Quincey

- **You are reading a book for an important class discussion in the morning when one of your friends comes over and asks you to go for a cup of coffee; you (circle the answer that best applies to you):**

    1. Tell your friend you can't go, you have to read
    2. Invite your friend in to talk
    3. Go with your friend for coffee, not thinking about the book
    4. Go with your friend for coffee, but have a poor time because you have to read
    5. Go with your friend for coffee, race back and read the book overnight
    6. Go with your friend for coffee and don't finish the book

    ☐ Yes   ☐ No      This is an issue for me.

    Because:

    _____

    _____

    _____

    _____

    _____

    Here is an idea how to change it:

    _____

    _____

    _____

    _____

# Am I a Procrastinator?

*"To be always intending to live a new life, but never to find time to set about it; this is as if a man should put off eating and drinking and sleeping from one day and night to another, till he is starved and destroyed."*

—John Tillotson

- **Do you think you have good study habits?**

☐ Yes   ☐ No       This is an issue for me.

Because:

_____

_____

_____

_____

_____

Here is an idea how to change it:

_____

_____

_____

_____

_____

# Am I a Procrastinator?

*"Nothing is ours except time."*

—Seneca

- **You have to study for a test being given in the morning, but there is a party going on next-door and you are having a hard time concentrating; you (circle the answer that best applies to you):**

    1. Knock on the door and ask them to quiet down
    2. Join the party for a few minutes
    3. Pack your things up and go somewhere quiet to study
    4. Stay put and try to get through it
    5. Wait until the party is over and begin studying at that time

    ☐ Yes    ☐ No     This is an issue for me.

Because:

_____

_____

_____

_____

_____

Here is an idea how to change it:

_____

_____

_____

_____

_____

# Am I a Procrastinator?

*"The leading rule for the lawyer, as for the man of every other calling, is diligence. Leave nothing for tomorrow which can be done today."*

—Abraham Lincoln

- You are working on a group assignment with one other person. The deadline for the presentation is in two weeks. You are not done with your part of the assignment. The other person is almost done; you (circle the answer that best applies to you):

  1. Ask for another week
  2. Talk to the other person about it immediately
  3. Ask for help
  4. Hope you get it done on time
  5. Talk to the other person a day before the presentation is due

  ☐ Yes   ☐ No      This is an issue for me.

  Because:

  _____

  _____

  _____

  _____

  _____

  Here is an idea how to change it:

  _____

  _____

  _____

  _____

  _____

# Am I a Procrastinator?

*"Do not boast about tomorrow for you don't know what a day may bring forth."*

—Proverbs 27:1

- **Using the study issues procrastination questions as a guide, list two of the most crucial situations that confronted you:**

_____

Situation #1

_____

Way in which you procrastinated

_____

Underlying reason for the procrastination

_____

What technique can you use to change for the future?




_____

Situation #2

_____

Way in which you procrastinated

_____

Underlying reason for the procrastination

_____

What technique can you use to change for the future?

# Am I a Procrastinator?

*"Delaying gratification is a process of scheduling the pain and pleasure of life in such way as to enhance the pleasure by meeting and experiencing the pain first and getting it over with. It is the only decent way to live."*

—M. Scott Peck

## Personal and Household Errands Procrastination

This section of the self-evaluation concentrates on the errands you do around the house.

- **Your car is supposed to have the oil changed every 3000 miles. You look at the odometer and notice that it is at 3050 since the last change; you (circle the answer that best applies to you):**

  1. Immediately take the car in for service
  2. Let it go a few more weeks
  3. Plan to service the car, but never seem to get it done
  4. Drive the car until the oil light goes on
  5. Call AAA because your car stopped on the freeway

  ☐ Yes   ☐ No      This is an issue for me.

  Because:

  _____

  _____

  _____

  _____

  _____

  Here is an idea how to change it:

  _____

  _____

  _____

  _____

  _____

# Am I a Procrastinator?

*"The really happy people are those who have broken the chains of procrastination, those who find satisfaction in doing the job at hand. They're full of eagerness, zest, productivity. You can be, too."*

—Norman Vincent Peale

- **When you go to the store, you (circle the answer that best applies to you):**

  1. Write out a list of the items you need
  2. Try to remember what you need
  3. Walk up and down each aisle buying what you need
  4. Often forget to bring home the items you need

  ☐ Yes   ☐ No      This is an issue for me.

Because:

_____

_____

_____

_____

_____

Here is an idea how to change it:

_____

_____

_____

_____

_____

# Am I a Procrastinator?

*"Today is the wise man's day, tomorrow is the fool's day. The wise man is the one when he sees what ought to be done, does it today. The foolish man, when he sees what ought to be done, says, 'I will do it tomorrow.'"*

—Unknown

- **Have you ever put off a home repair that later ended up costing you more than the original repair?**

    ☐ Yes   ☐ No       This is an issue for me.

    Because:

    _____

    _____

    _____

    _____

    _____

    Here is an idea how to change it:

    _____

    _____

    _____

    _____

    _____

# Am I a Procrastinator?

*"Do not put your work off till tomorrow and the day after; for a sluggish worker does not fill his barn, nor one who puts off his work; industry makes work go well, but a man who puts off work is always at hand-grips with ruin."*

—Hesiod

- **Would you say that you mow your lawn (circle the answer that best applies to you):**

    1. Once a week during growing season
    2. When it needs it
    3. You never seem to get around to it
    4. You have a gardener

    ☐ Yes  ☐ No    This is an issue for me.

    Because:

    _____

    _____

    _____

    _____

    _____

    Here is an idea how to change it:

    _____

    _____

    _____

    _____

# Am I a Procrastinator?

*"To be always intending to make a new and better life but never to find time to set about it is as to put off eating and drinking and sleeping from one day to the next until you're dead."*

—Og Mandino

- **Would you say that you get your hair cut or styled (circle the answer that best applies to you):**

    1. The same time, every time
    2. When it needs it
    3. When I can't stand it
    4. When it's been too long

    ☐ Yes    ☐ No      This is an issue for me.

    Because:

    _____

    _____

    _____

    _____

    _____

    Here is an idea how to change it:

    _____

    _____

    _____

    _____

    _____

# Am I a Procrastinator?

*"We shall never have more time. We have, and have always had, all the time there is. No object is served in waiting until next week or even until tomorrow. Keep going day in and day out. Concentrate on something useful. Having decided to achieve a task, achieve it at all costs."*

—Arnold Bennett

- **Concerning your home repairs, do you (circle the answer that best applies to you):**

    1. Write a list of repairs that need to be done and when
    2. Fix or get them fixed as you notice them
    3. Fix or get them fixed when you're told to
    4. Fix or get them fixed after they have broken

    ☐ Yes      ☐ No      This is an issue for me.

    Because:

    _____

    _____

    _____

    _____

    _____

    Here is an idea how to change it:

    _____

    _____

    _____

    _____

    _____

# Am I a Procrastinator?

*"The secret of getting ahead is getting started. The secret of getting started is breaking your complex overwhelming tasks into small manageable tasks, and then starting on the first one."*

—Mark Twain

- Using the household errands procrastination questions as a guide, list two of the most crucial situations that confronted you:

_____

Situation #1

_____

Way in which you procrastinated

_____

Underlying reason for the procrastination

_____

What technique can you use to change for the future?

_____

Situation #2

_____

Way in which you procrastinated

_____

Underlying reason for the procrastination

_____

What technique can you use to change for the future?

# Tools for Change

*"Procrastination is, hands down, our favorite form of self-sabotage."*
—**Alyce P. Cornyn-Selby**

Now that you have worked with the interactive sections of this workbook, it is now time to get some useful tips that will help you organize your life.

This section breaks down several common tasks into steps. It is not meant to be an exhaustive listing. It does, however, demonstrate the process of breaking down projects into the tasks that can be completed.

# Tools for Change

*"You may never know what results will come from your action. But if you do nothing there will be no result."*

—Ganobi

## • Calendars

1. Determine if you need an electronic or paper calendar.
2. Determine if your handwriting is large or small in size to determine what size calendar pages you may need.
3. Decide if you are a "night" person or "morning" person and then create some time when you are most alert to plan tomorrow (and transfer items from yesterday which are not complete).
4. If this becomes overwhelming ask someone to sit with you and hold you accountable to complete the task the first few times.

## • Car Repair and Maintenance

1. Go out to your car only to make an assessment.
2. Make a list of all the things you've been meaning to do (peel gum off the back of the seat, replace broken side-view mirror, oil change).
3. Prioritize the list.
4. Begin first project.

## • CDs and DVDs

1. Gather all of your disks into one area.
2. Open each to confirm each disk is in the correct jewel case.
3. Get a shelf or other box large enough for all of the your disks and future disks to fit.
4. Put them in an order of your choice (alphabetical or by category).
5. As you play them put them near your music center.
6. When you are done playing a disk, return it to its place.

## • Closets and Garages

1. Select a date to organize.
2. Ask one or more people to join you.
3. Make sure you begin and complete the task in one day.
4. Stay away from details.

# Tools for Change

*"He that is good for making excuses is seldom good for anything else."*
—*Benjamin Franklin*

- ## Contacts and Addresses
  1. Gather all business cards and small slips of papers with addresses and phone number from around the house or the office.
  2. Once bunched together, sort the enormous pile into alphabetical piles.
  3. Rubber band all the "A" contacts, "B" contacts, "C" contacts.
  4. Enlist help to have the cards typed into your contact list or written into your address book.

- ## Desk
  1. If your intention is to organize the desk, you must focus on that task only (not file drawers or supply shelves, or returning e-mails). Organize the desk.
  2. Enroll a colleague's or family member's help and agree on the amount of time you will spend on this project and set a timer.
  3. Collect all the papers from all over the desk and make just one pile.
  4. Begin sorting that huge stack of papers into categories (don't sign anything, don't flip through a journal), just sort by category—bills with bills, kids' artwork with kids' artwork.
  5. Decide which of the piles is most important.
  6. Make an appointment with yourself (in your calendar) to work on the important pile.

- ## Doctor's Appointments
  1. Tell a friend or family member that you need to make a doctor's appointment and ask them if they would be willing to hold you accountable for keeping it.
  2. Once you've selected a friend, make the appointment with your doctor.
  3. Inform your friend of the appointment date and ask them to call you the night before or the morning of the appointment.
  4. Prepare yourself for a positive experience (take a book to read while waiting, have a list of what the reasons are for your appointment, take an active role in understanding what you learn about yourself from your doctor (ask questions).

- ## Exercise
  1. Confirm with your doctor that you are able to exercise.
  2. Set a goal (weight loss, heart strengthening, building bulk).
  3. Choose a time, duration and frequency for your exercise (start slowly).
  4. If possible exercise with a friend to encourage each other.

# Tools for Change

*"You pile up enough tomorrows, and you'll find you've collected a lot of empty yesterdays."*

**—Professor Harrold Hill (The Music Man)**

## • Gift Giving

1. Make a list of all the people you generally buy gifts for and keep it in your calendar.
2. Keep sizes, favorite colors, preferences next to each name.
3. Decide on a gift-giving theme: Everyone shall receive books, or everyone shall receive something hand made, or everyone shall receive gift certificates (whether it's for a holiday, or birthday, male or female). This limits the indecision before these events occur.

## • Heirlooms

1. Unless you are using them or already displaying them, bring all heirlooms together in one room (if possible).
2. Sort like items with like items.
3. Ask yourself the story behind each "collection." If it's a meaningful piece or collection, keep it! If not, but you feel an obligation to keep it, consider taking a photo of yourself and the family with the heirloom and frame the memory and let the piece or the collection "go."

## • Holidays

1. Pull out your calendar right now.
2. Decide which holidays you plan to celebrate and log these in your calendar.
3. Assign time prior to each of those holidays to prepare for it (example: Memorial Day—you may wish to camp—make an appointment with yourself a month prior to organize the gear and get it out of the garage).

## • House Cleaning

1. Pick the most difficult area and make a list of the "to dos."
2. Enlist two others for help.
3. Post the list and assign each of you to the tasks.
4. Select outrageously fun music.

## • Magazines

1. Collect magazines from all over the house, car and office.
2. Sort like subscriptions together.
3. Place the cooking magazines in the kitchen, travel and leisure perhaps in the bedroom or welding world at the workbench.
4. Set a time boundary for yourself—if I don't read my magazines within three months, I'm giving them to the local hospital.

# Tools for Change

*"In any moment of decision the best thing you can do is the right thing, the next best thing is the wrong thing, and the worst thing you can do is nothing."*
**—Theodore Roosevelt**

- ## Mail and E-mail
  1. Set up your spam protection.
  2. If your program allows, create an "action required" folder.
  3. When you receive an e-mail, read it, if action is required, put it in the folder.
  4. If the person who sent it is important to you, save the e-mail address.
  5. If no action is required and you don't need to save the e-mail, delete it.

- ## Memorabilia
  1. Collect all memorabilia from all parts of the house and office.
  2. Sort memorabilia by person or event.
  3. Ask yourself what is the story behind each piece. If it is truly meaningful prepare to store it or display it.
  4. Designate a memorabilia section in your home or office which is clean and dry.
  5. Store memorabilia in protective containers in the designated areas.

- ## Photographs
  1. Gather your photographs from all over the house.
  2. Decide how you like to look at photos (computer, albums, individually)
  3. Group your photos in categories like people or events.

- ## Returning Purchased Items
  1. Gather all items which need to be returned.
  2. Sort items by purchase or gift location. (Department store or hardware store . . .)
  3. Designate an "items to be returned" section in your home or office.
  4. Match all receipts to returnable items.
  5. Make a new commitment to purchase items only listed on your shopping list—avoiding all impulse buys or multiple purchases.

- ## Thank-You Notes
  1. Avoid perfection at all costs.
  2. Less is more (one sentence is just great)!
  3. Once the envelope is addressed, have someone *else* mail it for you.

# Forms for Change

*"There are those of us who are always about to live. We are waiting until things change, until there is more time, until we are less tired, until we get a promotion, until we settle down—until, until, until. It always seems as if there is some major event that must occur in our lives before we begin living."*

—George Sheehan

The following section provides you forms and lists to help you organize your life. Remember, as Dr. Ferrari says, procrastination is not a time management problem. These forms are here to help you organize. They are not the sole answer to your procrastination.

You may copy these forms for your use or download them from *www.hci-online.com/makeover.*

# Prioritization Chart™

Word for the Day _____ Date _____

| Weight: _____ <br> Exercise: | | | Most Important Tasks: |
|---|---|---|---|

**Food Log**

| Breakfast | Lunch | Dinner | To Do: |
|---|---|---|---|
| | | | |

| Success Questions: <br> 1. <br> 2. <br> 3. <br> 4. <br> 5. | What can I delete from my day? |
|---|---|

| Purchases | 6:00 | | 1:30 | |
|---|---|---|---|---|
| | 6:30 | | 2:00 | |
| | 7:00 | | 2:30 | |
| | 7:30 | | 3:00 | |
| | 8:00 | | 3:30 | |
| | 8:30 | | 4:00 | |
| | 9:00 | | 4:30 | |
| Expenses | 9:30 | | 5:00 | |
| | 10:00 | | 5:30 | |
| | 10:30 | | 6:00 | |
| | 11:00 | | 6:30 | |
| | 11:30 | | 7:00 | |
| | 12:00 | | 7:30 | |
| | 12:30 | | 8:00 | |
| | 1:00 | | 8:30 | |

# Procrastination Projects List

List all projects in each area and prioritize them.

## Health and Fitness

| Task | Priority |
|------|----------|
| _____ | _____ |
| _____ | _____ |
| _____ | _____ |
| _____ | _____ |
| _____ | _____ |

## Recreation and Travel

| Task | Priority |
|------|----------|
| _____ | _____ |
| _____ | _____ |
| _____ | _____ |
| _____ | _____ |
| _____ | _____ |

## Finance

| Task | Priority |
|------|----------|
| _____ | _____ |
| _____ | _____ |
| _____ | _____ |
| _____ | _____ |

## Wardrobe

| Task | Priority |
|------|----------|
| _____ | _____ |
| _____ | _____ |
| _____ | _____ |
| _____ | _____ |

## Car, Home, Apartment

| Task | Priority |
|------|----------|
| _____ | _____ |
| _____ | _____ |
| _____ | _____ |

## Spirituality

| Task | Priority |
|------|----------|
| _____ | _____ |
| _____ | _____ |
| _____ | _____ |

# Procrastination Projects List

List all projects in each area and prioritize them.

## Relationships

| Task | Priority |
|------|----------|
|  |  |
|  |  |
|  |  |
|  |  |
|  |  |

| Task | Priority |
|------|----------|
|  |  |
|  |  |
|  |  |
|  |  |
|  |  |

| Task | Priority |
|------|----------|
|  |  |
|  |  |
|  |  |
|  |  |

## Education

| Task | Priority |
|------|----------|
|  |  |
|  |  |
|  |  |
|  |  |
|  |  |

| Task | Priority |
|------|----------|
|  |  |
|  |  |
|  |  |
|  |  |
|  |  |

| Task | Priority |
|------|----------|
|  |  |
|  |  |
|  |  |
|  |  |

# Top Project Completion Form

Select two top projects from the Procrastination List. Use this form to help you organize the project. Be sure to include how long you think it will take to complete the task. Be as honest with yourself as possible.

## Top Project #1:

| Ten Steps | Completion Time (Hours: Minutes) |
|---|---|
| 1. _____ | |
| 2. _____ | |
| 3. _____ | |
| 4. _____ | |
| 5. _____ | |
| 6. _____ | |
| 7. _____ | |
| 8. _____ | |
| 9. _____ | |
| 10. _____ | |

Total Time Necessary to complete this project: _____

## Enter these steps into your calendar!

_____    _____
Signature                                                              Date

# Top Project Completion Form

Select two top projects from the Procrastination List. Use this form to help you organize the project. Be sure to include how long you think it will take to complete the task. Be as honest with yourself as possible.

## Top Project #2:

_____

| Ten Steps | Completion Time (Hours: Minutes) |

1. _____

2. _____

3. _____

4. _____

5. _____

6. _____

7. _____

8. _____

9. _____

10. _____

Total Time Necessary to complete this project: _____

## Enter these steps into your calendar!

_____        _____
Signature                                                    Date

# To Do List

To Be Completed by: _____ Deadline: _____

| Done? | Project 1 | Due By? | Notes |
|---|---|---|---|
| | Planning | | |
| | Preparation | | |
| | Task A | | |
| | Task B | | |
| | Task C | | |
| | Task D | | |
| | Paperwork | | |
| | Hand-off | | |
| | Follow-up | | |

| Done? | Project 2 | Due By? | Notes |
|---|---|---|---|
| | Planning | | |
| | Preparation | | |
| | Task A | | |
| | Task B | | |
| | Task C | | |
| | Task D | | |
| | Paperwork | | |
| | Hand-off | | |
| | Follow-up | | |

| Done? | Project 3 | Due By? | Notes |
|---|---|---|---|
| | Planning | | |
| | Preparation | | |
| | Task A | | |
| | Task B | | |
| | Task C | | |
| | Task D | | |
| | Paperwork | | |
| | Hand-off | | |
| | Follow-up | | |

# To Do List

Emphasis _____ Date _____

**Item**                                                                    **Priority**

1. _____    _____

2. _____    _____

3. _____    _____

4. _____    _____

5. _____    _____

6. _____    _____

7. _____    _____

8. _____    _____

9. _____    _____

10. _____    _____

11. _____    _____

12. _____    _____

13. _____    _____

14. _____    _____

15. _____    _____

16. _____    _____

17. _____    _____

18. _____    _____

# Weekly Planner

Use this form to plan your week.

| | Monday | Tuesday | Wednesday | Thursday | Friday | Saturday | Sunday |
|---|---|---|---|---|---|---|---|
| 5:30 am | | | | | | | |
| 6:00 am | | | | | | | |
| 6:30 am | | | | | | | |
| 7:00 am | | | | | | | |
| 7:30 am | | | | | | | |
| 8:00 am | | | | | | | |
| 8:30 am | | | | | | | |
| 9:00 am | | | | | | | |
| 9:30 am | | | | | | | |
| 10:00 am | | | | | | | |
| 10:30 am | | | | | | | |
| 11:00 am | | | | | | | |
| 11:30 am | | | | | | | |
| 12:00 pm | | | | | | | |
| 12:30 pm | | | | | | | |
| 1:00 pm | | | | | | | |
| 1:30 pm | | | | | | | |
| 2:00 pm | | | | | | | |
| 2:30 pm | | | | | | | |
| 3:00 pm | | | | | | | |
| 3:30 pm | | | | | | | |
| 4:00 pm | | | | | | | |
| 4:30 pm | | | | | | | |
| 5:00 pm | | | | | | | |
| 5:30 pm | | | | | | | |
| 6:00 pm | | | | | | | |
| 6:30 pm | | | | | | | |
| 7:00 pm | | | | | | | |
| 7:30 pm | | | | | | | |
| 8:00 pm | | | | | | | |
| 8:30 pm | | | | | | | |
| 9:00 pm | | | | | | | |
| 9:30 pm | | | | | | | |
| 10:00 pm | | | | | | | |
| 10:30 pm | | | | | | | |
| 11:00 pm | | | | | | | |
| 11:30 pm | | | | | | | |

# Medical History "A"

Use this form to keep track of information that could help you in a medical situation.

| | | |
|---|---|---|
| Last Name | First Name | Middle |

| | | | |
|---|---|---|---|
| Address | City | State | Zip |

| | | | |
|---|---|---|---|
| Home Phone | Business Phone | Mobile Phone | Other Phone |

I Am Under the Care Of:

Dr. _____

                             Reason                         Phone

Dr. _____

                             Reason                         Phone

Dr. _____

                             Reason                         Phone

## Medications I Am Taking:

| Name | Dosage |
|---|---|
| | |
| | |
| | |

## All Surgeries:

## All Allergies:

# Medical History "B"

Use this form to keep track of information that could help you in a medical situation.

Mother's History:

_____

_____

_____

_____

_____

_____

_____

Father's History:

_____

_____

_____

_____

_____

_____

_____

# Financial Document Locator

It is easy to procrastinate if you can't find the documents you need to get your work done. The following is a form to help you locate your important financial documents.

| Document(s) | Location |
|---|---|
| Checks, statements and other banking papers | _____ |
| Stocks, bonds and mutual fund certificates | _____ |
| Deeds | _____ |
| Trust documents | _____ |
| Loan statements and payment books | _____ |
| Home rental or ownership papers | _____ |
| Automobile titles | _____ |
| Insurance policies | _____ |
| Pension papers | _____ |
| Wills | _____ |
| Prior tax returns | _____ |
| Tax receipts | _____ |
| Active tax papers | _____ |
| _____ | _____ |
| _____ | _____ |
| _____ | _____ |
| _____ | _____ |

# Event Budgeting

Event Title_____ Date: _____

This form will help you track expenses for parties and other events

| Expenses | | | |
|---|---|---|---|
| **Location** | **Description** | **Estimated** | **Actual** |
| Room and hall fees | | | |
| Site Staff | | | |
| Equipment | | | |
| Tables and chairs | | | |
| Other | | | |
| Other | | | |
| **Location Subtotal** | | | |
| **Decorations** | **Description** | **Estimated** | **Actual** |
| Flowers | | | |
| Candles | | | |
| Lighting | | | |
| Balloons | | | |
| Paper Supplies | | | |
| Other | | | |
| Other | | | |
| **Decorations Subtotal** | | | |
| **Publicity** | **Description** | **Estimated** | **Actual** |
| Graphic Work | | | |
| Photocopying/Printing | | | |
| Postage | | | |
| Other | | | |
| Other | | | |
| **Publicity Subtotal** | | | |
| **Refreshments** | **Description** | **Estimated** | **Actual** |
| Food | | | |
| Drink | | | |
| Linens | | | |
| Staff and Gratuities | | | |
| Other | | | |
| Other | | | |
| **Refreshments Subtotal** | | | |
| **Program** | **Description** | **Estimated** | **Actual** |
| Performers | | | |
| Speakers | | | |
| Travel | | | |
| Hotel | | | |
| Other | | | |
| Other | | | |
| **Program Subtotal** | | | |
| **Prizes** | **Description** | **Estimated** | **Actual** |
| Ribbons/Plaques/Trophies | | | |
| Gifts | | | |
| Other | | | |
| **Prizes Subtotal** | | | |
| **Miscellaneous** | **Description** | **Estimated** | **Actual** |
| Telephone | | | |
| Transportation | | | |
| Stationary Supplies | | | |
| Fax Services | | | |
| Other | | | |
| **Miscellaneous Subtotal** | | | |
| **Grand Total** | | | |

# Grocery List

Date _____

| Done | Produce | Quantity | Brand |
|------|---------|----------|-------|
|      |         |          |       |
|      |         |          |       |
|      |         |          |       |
|      |         |          |       |
|      |         |          |       |
|      |         |          |       |
|      |         |          |       |
|      |         |          |       |
|      |         |          |       |
|      |         |          |       |
|      |         |          |       |

| Done | Dairy | Quantity | Brand |
|------|-------|----------|-------|
|      |       |          |       |
|      |       |          |       |
|      |       |          |       |
|      |       |          |       |
|      |       |          |       |
|      |       |          |       |
|      |       |          |       |

| Done | Meat | Quantity | Brand |
|------|------|----------|-------|
|      |      |          |       |
|      |      |          |       |
|      |      |          |       |
|      |      |          |       |
|      |      |          |       |

| Done | Drinks | Quantity | Brand |
|------|--------|----------|-------|
|      |        |          |       |
|      |        |          |       |
|      |        |          |       |
|      |        |          |       |
|      |        |          |       |
|      |        |          |       |

# Grocery List

Date _____

| Done | Supplies | Quantity | Brand |
|------|----------|----------|-------|
|      |          |          |       |
|      |          |          |       |
|      |          |          |       |
|      |          |          |       |
|      |          |          |       |

| Done | Pasta | Quantity | Brand |
|------|-------|----------|-------|
|      |       |          |       |
|      |       |          |       |
|      |       |          |       |

| Done | Soup | Quantity | Brand |
|------|------|----------|-------|
|      |      |          |       |
|      |      |          |       |
|      |      |          |       |

| Done | Bakery | Quantity | Brand |
|------|--------|----------|-------|
|      |        |          |       |
|      |        |          |       |
|      |        |          |       |
|      |        |          |       |
|      |        |          |       |

| Done | Snacks | Quantity | Brand |
|------|--------|----------|-------|
|      |        |          |       |
|      |        |          |       |
|      |        |          |       |
|      |        |          |       |
|      |        |          |       |
|      |        |          |       |

| Done | Miscellaneous | Quantity | Brand |
|------|---------------|----------|-------|
|      |               |          |       |
|      |               |          |       |
|      |               |          |       |
|      |               |          |       |
|      |               |          |       |

153

# Grocery List

Date _____

| Done | Item | Quantity | Brand |
|------|------|----------|-------|
|      |      |          |       |
|      |      |          |       |
|      |      |          |       |
|      |      |          |       |
|      |      |          |       |
|      |      |          |       |
|      |      |          |       |
|      |      |          |       |
|      |      |          |       |
|      |      |          |       |
|      |      |          |       |
|      |      |          |       |
|      |      |          |       |
|      |      |          |       |
|      |      |          |       |
|      |      |          |       |
|      |      |          |       |
|      |      |          |       |
|      |      |          |       |
|      |      |          |       |
|      |      |          |       |
|      |      |          |       |
|      |      |          |       |
|      |      |          |       |
|      |      |          |       |
|      |      |          |       |
|      |      |          |       |
|      |      |          |       |
|      |      |          |       |
|      |      |          |       |
|      |      |          |       |
|      |      |          |       |
|      |      |          |       |
|      |      |          |       |
|      |      |          |       |
|      |      |          |       |
|      |      |          |       |
|      |      |          |       |
|      |      |          |       |
|      |      |          |       |

# Dates to Remember

| Date | Name of Person | Occasion | Comment |
| --- | --- | --- | --- |
| | | | |
| | | | |
| | | | |
| | | | |
| | | | |
| | | | |
| | | | |
| | | | |
| | | | |
| | | | |
| | | | |
| | | | |
| | | | |
| | | | |
| | | | |
| | | | |
| | | | |
| | | | |
| | | | |
| | | | |
| | | | |
| | | | |
| | | | |
| | | | |

# Resources

*"While we are postponing, life speeds by."*

—Seneca

We hope that you have benefited from your experience with this workbook.

We have included resources that we feel will help you as you continue to use your time more efficiently and conquer procrastination.

Feel free to investigate the information as fully as possible.

# Resources

*"The surest way to be late is to have plenty of time."*

—Leo Kennedy

**Business Resources**
*101 Ways to Promote Yourself: Tricks of the Trade for Taking Charge of Your Own Success*
By Raleigh Pinskey
Publisher: Avon (July 1, 1997)

I Could Do Anything If I Only Knew What It Was : How to Discover What You Really Want and How to Get It
by Barbara Sher
Publisher: Dell (August 5, 1995)

*Re-imagine!*
by Tom Peters
Publisher: Dorling Kindersley Publishing: First edition (October 1, 2003)

**Calendars**
At-A-Glance
(888) 302-4155

DayRunner
(800) 232-9786

DayTimer
(800) 225-5005

Franklin Covey
(800) 842-2439

Planner Pads Company
(800)315-7526

**Car Repair**
AAA (American Automobile Association)
www.aaa.com

**Credit Reporting Agencies**
Equifax (800) 525-6285
Experien (Formerly TRW) (888) 397-3742
Trans Union (800) 680-7289

**Closets and Garages**
Astech Closet Systems
www.astechclosets.com

California Closets
(415) 453-7900
khofmann@calclosets.com

CLOSETS Magazine
Lincolnshire, IL
(800) 343-2016
www.closetsmagazine.com

Closet & Storage Concepts
Voorhees, NJ
www.closetandstorageconcepts.com

Closet Factory
(281) 355-7676
closet@wt.net

Closet Factory
Washington DC
(301) 893-1605
dennycs@comcast.net

Closet Factory
Carrollton, TX
www.closetfactory.com

The Closet Lady Inc
New York, NY
www.closetlady.com

Garage Squad Inc
Blaine, MN

GarageTek
Syosset, NY
www.garagetek.com

GarageTek
Mossville, IL
(309) 579-2929
rledford@garagetek.com

GarageTek
Berthoud, CO
(970) 532-2800

GarageTek
Rockville, MD
(703) 425-0900
jfrank@garagetek.com

GarageTek
Dallas, TX
(214) 451-3400

# Resources

*"The next day is never so good as the day before."*

—Syrus

Gladiator Garage Works by Whirlpool Corp
Benton Harbor, MI
wwww.gladiatorgw.com

The Uncluttered Garage Inc
Las Flores, CA
www.unclutteredgarage.com

## Financial
CheckFree Corp.
(678) 375-1595
jdwicks@checkfree.com

*New Century Family Money Book*
By Jonathan Pond
Publisher: Delacorte Press (March 1, 1993)

Financial Support Services
(314) 721-1375
checksinc@mindspring.com

Investor's Central Communications, Inc
(717) 336-2479
www.iccominc.com

Internal Revenue Service
Forms and Assistance
www.irs.gov/formspubs/

The Tax Tracker LLC
Hartford, CT
www.taxtracker.com

## Home
1-800-Got-Junk?
www.1800gotjunk.com

Container Store
(800) 733-3532

Get Organized
(800) 803-9400

Exposures
(800) 572-5750

Frontgate
(800) 626-6488

Hold Everything
(800) 421-2264

IKEA
(888) 225-IKEA

Pottery Barn
(800) 922-5507

Public Storage
(800) 44-Store

Trifles Spaces
(800) 456-7019

## Medical
*52 Simple Steps to Natural Health*
By Mark Mayell
Publisher: Pocket (July 1, 1997)

Senior Organizer
www.biobinders.com
(800) 791-8071

## Memorabilia
Cherished Memories—The Story of My Life
www.biobinders.com
(800) 791-8071

## Office
20-20 Technologies Inc
www.2020design.com

Bindertek
(800) 456-3453

Cardinal Brands Inc
www.cardinalbrands.com

Fujitsu Computer Products of America
(408) 236-3070

Levenger
(800) 544-0880

Mobile Office Outfitter
(800) 426-3453

Office Depot
(800) 685-8800

# Resources

*"Postpone not your life."*

—Ralph Waldo Emerson

Office Max
(800) 788-8080

Reliable Home Office
(800) 869-6000

Scanalog Inc.
(845) 279-7550
scanalog.com

Staples
(800) 333-3330

Ultimate Office Inc
Farmingdale, NJ
www.ultoffice.com

**Organizing Products
and Services**
Cableorganizer.com
(877) 547-4580
www.cableorganizer.com

Center for Organization and Goal Planning
(800) 860-GOAL
www.centerfororganization.com

Container Store
Coppell, TX
(888) CON-TAIN

Delphi Health Products Inc
www.biobinders.com
(800) 791-8071

Esselte Corporation
Melville, NY
www.esselteamericas.com

Find Every File
(877) 701-2594
www.findeveryfile.com

Knape & Vogt Manufacturing Co
Grand Rapids, MI
www.kv.com

Lillian Vernon Corporation
(914) 925-1300
www.lillianvernon.com

Find Every File
(877) 701-2594
www.findeveryfile.com

MeadWestvaco Consumer & Office Products
Sidney, NY
www.at-a-glance.com

Newell Rubbermaid Sanford Division
(708) 240-3894

Online Organizing.com
(404) 607-7857
www.onlineorganizing.com

Organize Everything Inc
www.organize-everything.com

Organized From the Start Inc—BabyBriefcase
(888) 584-2337
www.organizedfromthestart.com

Organized Living
Lenexa, KS
www.organizedliving.com

PSD Office
Rapid City, SD
www.psdoffice.com

Purseket
(914) 921-2907
nancyjane.carson@verizon.net

Rubbermaid Home Products
Fairlawn, OH
(888) 895-2110

SCHULTE Corporation
Cincinnati, OH
www.schultestorage.com

Simpliciti Inc
San Clemente, CA
(800) 732-8091

Smead Manufacturing Company
(651) 438-2055
www.smead.com

*"Wasted days can never be recalled."*

—**Anonymous**

UniKeep LLC
Marysville, OH
(937) 645-4675

WallPerfect
Gulf Breeze, FL
www.wallperfect.com

Windquest Companies Inc
Holland, MI
www.windquestco.com

**Paper Management**
*Taming the Paper Tiger*
Barbara Hemphill, Random House 1997

**Relationships**
CODA (Co-Dependents Anonymous)
www.codependents.org/

*The Dance of Anger: A Woman's Guide to Changing the Patterns of Intimate Relationships*
by Harriet Lerner
Publisher: Quill; Reissue edition (1997)

*He's Just Not that Into You: The No-Excuses Truth to Understanding Guys*
by Greg Behrendt, Liz Tuccillo
Publisher: Simon Spotlight Entertainment
(September 1, 2004)

*How to Say No Without Feeling Guilty : And Say Yes to More Time, and What Matters Most to You*
by Patti Breitman, Connie Hatch
Publisher: Broadway (February 13, 2001)

*Making Peace with Your Parents*
by Harold Bloomfield, MD Leonard Felder, PHD
Publisher: Ballantine Books; Reissue edition
(September 29, 1996)

**Recycling**
AuctionDrop
San Carlos, CA

**Space Design**
Creative Workspaces
Oceanside, CA
(760) 758-2238
skoretke@creativeworkspaces.com

JRE Home & Office Designs
Huntingdon Valley, PA

Madison 300 Interiors
(201) 779-8903
madison300@comcast.net

Market House Kitchen & Bath
Lees Summit, MO
mj@market-house.net

Murphy Beds by New Harmony Bedrooms, Inc
(978) 327-6512
www.murphywallbeds.com

Refined Spaces Inc
(248) 249-1971
refinedspacesinc@yahoo.com

Rev-A-Shelf
Louisville, KY
www.rev-a-shelf.com

Shelving Inc
(248) 852-8600
joe@shelving.com

Space Savers
Winston-Salem, NC
(800) 849-7210

Western School of Feng Shui
Solana Beach, CA
www.wsfs.com

**Support Systems Resources**
AA (Alcoholics Anonymous)
www.alchoholics-anonymous.org

CLA (Clutters' Anonymous)
www.cluttersanonymous.net

Debtors Anonymous
www.debtorsanonoymous.org

FA (Food Addicts in Recovery)
www.foodaddicts.org

*Feel the Fear and Do It Anyway*
By Susan Jeffers
Publisher: Ballantine Books; Reissue edition
(April 12, 1988)

# Resources

*"Do not wait for the last judgment. It takes place every day."*

—Albert Camus

**Support Systems (cont'd.)**
NAPO (National Association of Professional Organizers)
www.napo.net

NSGCD (National Study Group on Chronic Disorganization)
www.nsgcd.org

Sharma Bennett
Licensed Psychotheropist—Indviduals, Couples and Families
(310) 967-5048

*When I Roll Out of Bed Tomorrow Morning, I Just Want to Be
Happy . . .*
(365 Day Series) [Illustrated] by Dorothy K. Breininger
Center for Organization & Goal Planning; First edition
edition (2004)

# About the Authors

**Dorothy K. Breininger**, the CEO of the Center for Organization and Goal Planning, coaches CEOs, high profile celebrities, business entrepreneurs and homemakers on how to conquer procrastination while developing a fulfilling work and home life. A sought-after international speaker, Dorothy serves as a board director for the National Association of Professional Organizers, is a member of the National Association of Female Executives and has appeared on NBC's *Today Show,* the *Dr. Phil* show and has been featured in the *Los Angeles Times, Forbes Magazine* and *Better Homes and Gardens.* For more information on Dorothy, please visit: *www.centerfororganization.com.*

**Debby S. Bitticks**, CEO of Delphi Health Products, Inc., has recently co-authored *Cherished Memories—The Story of My Life* which chronicles the journey of one's life and *Senior Organizer* to guide a senior or a family member in tracking their medical, financial, legal and daily care plans. Debby has presented and spoken at the National Council on the Aging in Washington D.C. on intergenerational care and has appeared on CNN Financial News, CBS and other cable TV shows, as well as giving numerous national radio interviews. She has received the Blue Chip Enterprise Award given by the U.S. Chamber of Commerce and Connecticut Mutual Life Insurance Company. For more information on Debby, please visit: *www.biobinders.com.*

# Notes